SEASONAL SALADS
From Around the World

David Scott and Paddy Byrne

A Garden Way Publishing Book

STOREY COMMUNICATIONS, INC.
POWNAL, VERMONT 05261

NOTE

**Unless otherwise specified, all the recipes
in this book are for 4 people.**

First published in 1985 as *Seasonal Salads* by Ebury Press, The National Magazine
Company, Ltd., London. Copyright 1985 by David Scott and Paddy Byrne.

American adaptation by Linda Tilgner

"Growing A Salad Garden" was adapted from Tips for the Lazy Gardener
by Linda Tilgner (Garden Way Publishing © 1985).

Edited by Deborah Burns

Cover illustration by Sara Barbaris

Interior illustrations by Elayne Sears

U.S. edition copyright 1986 by Storey Communications, Inc.

First U.S. Edition

The name Garden Way Publishing is licensed to Storey Communications, Inc. by Garden Way, Inc.

Printed in the United States by Alpine Press

First printing, March 1986

Library of Congress Catalog Card Number: 85-45606

International Standard Book Number: 0-88266-418-2

Library of Congress Cataloging-in-Publication Data
Scott, David, 1944-
  Seasonal salads.
    I. Salads. I. Byrne, Paddy. II. Title.
TX807.S38 1986   641-8'3   85-45606
ISBN 0-88266-418-2 (pbk.)

Contents

v   Preface to the American Edition

vi   Preface to the British Edition

1   Introduction

5   Useful Kitchen Equipment

8   Oils and Vinegars

10   Buying, Preparing, and Cooking Fresh Fruit and Vegetables

26   Pantry Essentials

28   Herbs, Spices, and Other Flavorings for Salads

35   Spring Salads

55   Summer Salads

78   Autumn Salads

96   Winter Salads

124   Dressings

142   Growing a Salad Garden

146   Seasonal Availability Chart

148   Index

Preface to the American Edition

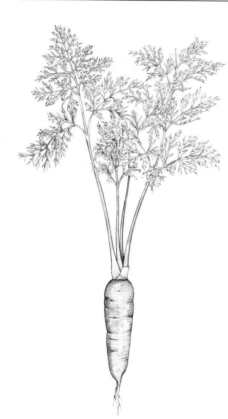

Seasonal Salads contains a fusion of culinary ideas from all parts of Europe, America, the Middle East, Japan, Indonesia, and many other places. The first edition, which was a great success, was written for the British market, but it was heavily influenced by the authors' travels. We hope this new American edition, with its many original fruit and vegetable combinations, tasty dressings, and new ideas for adventurous palates, will be a happy addition to the American diet.

The purpose of the book is to provide a selection of recipes for vegetables in their proper seasons. In season, vegetables taste better, do you more good, and cost less. This is true whether you shop in a small general store, a farmers' market, or a supermarket—or even if you "grow your own."

Every one of our recipes can be used by vegetarians, but they are also suitable for accompanying meat, fish, and poultry dishes. The salads may also form a delicious part of a healthy, high-fiber, low-fat diet.

Apart from the recipes, the book also offers expert advice on kitchen equipment, oils and vinegars, the essential stock cupboard, and how to buy, prepare and cook fresh fruits and vegetables.

David Scott and Paddy Byrne
Liverpool, November 1985

Preface to the British Edition

We have collected, adapted, and devised the recipes in this book over a period of fourteen years. During this time we have bought produce for and operated a large popular restaurant, which has established a fine reputation for its fresh salads. Our book contains ethnic recipes, classic combinations, many quite precise self-contained starter and side salads to accompany formal meals, and a good number of visually exciting, sometimes humorous, and above all, fine-tasting salads that you will not find elsewhere.

By presenting the salads seasonally, we trust we will save you time and money searching the shops for a vegetable that is quite out of season, only to be had at great expense or well past its best.

With few exceptions the recipes are simple, and we hope the book will provide a sound basis for your own creative salad making. Our aim is to show you that salad making can be an art just like sauce making or pâtisserie, only more so, since salad vegetables have shape and form, a great variety of color, and a multitude of textures. The essence of the art of salad making is to know the qualities of the raw materials, to judge how they can best be complemented and presented, and then to compose the salad accordingly. This process is the heart of this book, and we hope it will help you use your own creativity to produce a wide range of salads that do not just play a supporting role to fish, meat, or cheese, but make an equal contribution to a meal.

David Scott and Paddy Byrne
Liverpool, December 1984

Introduction

SALADS AND SEASONS

Outside the tropics, all vegetables have their seasons.

Because it is central to the theme of the book, we must emphasize that when we say a vegetable is in season we mean not only that it is available, but that it is at its tastiest and its cheapest as well. This is probably because it has been grown locally and is both fresh and plentiful. Prices will be further cut because costs of transport and packaging will be much reduced. By following our recipes season by season, you can save money on salad vegetables, and, we hope, enjoy better, more nutritional salads. And always remember that in order to enjoy fully the variety of short-season vegetables, you may sometimes have to push into another season any produce that you know is available over a longer period. Our hints on buying salad vegetables on pages 10 to 25 will be particularly useful in this regard.

DRESSINGS FOR SALADS

For most of our salads we have recommended a minimum quantity of dressing. This is for two reasons. First, we are using vegetables when their flavor is at its finest and thus we want to complement the taste, not to submerge it. Second, dressings usually contain oils and creams, and though we would not do without them, we want to use these fat-rich ingredients in moderation. See pages 124 to 141 for recipes.

Always taste dressings before pouring them over the vegetables. You may like them a little sweeter, sharper, or hotter than we do. Adjust them to your personal preferences—the recipes are certainly not sacrosanct. Another reason for tasting is that many ingredients are of variable strength, sweetness, and flavor—tomatoes, carrots, oranges, chilies, paprika, vinegars, and, above all, tamari are all unpredictable. You should test each new ingredient before you begin to prepare your salad.

GARNISHES

With thought and imagination, you can improvise garnishes to reflect individual salads both in appearance and in flavor. To us a garnish is an integral part of a salad, and much more than just a visual arrangement. There is nothing more boring than parsley scattered over everything. On the other hand, when the chosen vegetables are so carefully selected and cut that they look good from the first to last mouthful, salads are best presented ungarnished.

SEASONAL SALADS AND VEGETARIANS

Vegetarians can use every single one of our recipes, but we do not consider this book to be solely for them. Most of the recipes can stand on their own, but they will also be suitable for accompanying all types of meat, fish, eggs, and cheese dishes. Nevertheless, if this book results in the reader eating less meat, we would be well pleased.

SEASONAL SALADS FOR GOOD HEALTH

Most of our recipes could form part of a healthy, high-fiber, low-fat diet. Those few recipes with a high fat content are frequently accompanied by suggestions for low-fat alternatives. Conversely, some recipes low in fat may have suggestions to make them more appealing to those who like a richer diet. Nobody continues to eat food they dislike. People eating and enjoying their vegetables will gradually develop a healthier diet.

THE FRESHEST PRODUCE

The freshest, tastiest, and most nutritious vegetables come from your own garden. For tips on growing a salad garden outside your kitchen door, see page 142. And to find out when each fruit or vegetable is freshest and cheapest in the market, refer to the Seasonal Availability Chart on page 146.

GENERAL GUIDELINES
FOR SALAD MAKING

- Use only the very best and freshest ingredients.

- Be selective about what goes into a salad: a thoughtless collection of vegetables will appeal neither to the tongue nor to the eye. A great many salads are spoiled by the introduction of extra ingredients. Add nothing without considering how it will affect the final taste and appearance of the salad.

- Do not chop all salad ingredients uniformly, but respect the characteristic shape of each vegetable and how it is seen to its best advantage. This may mean cutting cabbage into long corrugated strips, cutting peppers into their sectional rings, cutting beef tomatoes horizontally to show off their wonderful "map-of-the-world" cross-sections, or leaving thin, twiglike green beans uncut. If you have several salads to prepare, see that you cut each in a different manner. Indeed, if you are presenting a large buffet, prepare some salads by hand and some by machine, to give even greater visual variety.

- Remember that strong-tasting vegetables like garlic or onions, used in small quantities as flavorings, should be chopped very finely in order to distribute their flavor evenly. Similarly, large, bland, starchy vegetables like potatoes should be cut or sliced small to enable the dressing to penetrate easily.

- Beware of unhappy combinations in which colors clash horribly (for example, tomato and beets, or radish and radicchio). Don't mix ingredients like celery and fennel, which look alike and crunch in a similar manner, or the effect on the taste buds will be reminiscent of tasting coffee when you thought you were about to taste tea. Beans, lentils, and other starchy foods are usually best served as separate salads, as they muddy the clean taste of more delicate ingredients.

- Many salads are valued for their crisp textures and sharp colors. It is therefore essential that ingredients are not overcooked, and that any green vegetables, once cooked, are quickly chilled under running or iced water, to arrest the cooking process and to preserve their texture and color.

- Season and mix salads adequately, although in the light of recent findings it may be wise to use salt with discretion. Those who salt their cooked meals well will obviously not enjoy unsalted salads. Cabbage, dried beans, lentils, and, of course, potatoes, all need more salt than most vegetables. Legumes need plenty of vinaigrette to give an edge to their earthy taste.

- Match dressings and solid ingredients carefully. For instance, a subtle dressing will be lost on a coarse-flavored legume or sharply flavored chicory, while strong dressings will swamp a delicate salad of lettuce or fresh, immature broad beans.

- Don't add too many different fresh herbs to your salads. All you are likely to do is overload and confuse the palate.

Useful Kitchen Equipment

The great majority of salads can be prepared using a minimum of good-quality kitchen equipment. One good, sharp knife is worth more than a rackful of inferior, blunt ones. With that premise in mind here are a few comments on some of the equipment we have found essential in our kitchens and at home.

Blenders. Electric blenders are extremely useful. With their help dressings can be made in seconds, whole egg mayonnaise is made with ease, and the preparation time of many dishes is radically reduced.

Chopping boards. A chopping board is essential for convenience, accident-free cutting, protection of kitchen surfaces, and extending the lives of knife edges. Hardwoods such as maple or yellow birch are the best.

Cookware. If you can afford stainless steel cookware, buy it. Stainless steel is robust and very easy to clean. Enamelware is equally good for cooking, but it will chip, leaving the base iron exposed. Even the enameled cast ironware will eventually wear out. Aluminum or uncoated ironware taints or discolors many vegetables and sauces. Forget about non-stick pans; the coating seldom remains intact for long and you're left with a thin, inferior aluminum pan.

Food processor. A food processor does most of the tasks a blender does. It will also grate and slice vegetables. This is a very useful asset if you wish to produce economical salads in winter and early spring. If you make lots of soups as well as salads this would be your ideal kitchen aid. Good ones are expensive.

Garlic press. Buy a large garlic press so that the cloves are squeezed through the grid rather than out around the edges of the press. Also useful for juicing fresh ginger and fresh chilies.

Jelly bag. A traditional jelly bag is ideal for straining excess liquid from overwatery yogurt. A piece of muslin makes a good substitute.

Kitchen scale. It is quickest to measure your produce by weight, rather than by stuffing it into a measuring cup.

Knife sharpener. A steel knife sharpener or oilstone (best of all for stainless steel knives) is a must. There is nothing more time consuming or frustrating than working with a blunt knife. Blunt knives are more likely to slip and cause accidents as you have to use so much more force behind them than if the cutting edge was sharp.

If you are on very good terms with your butcher, he may sharpen or even regrind your knives when necessary.

Knives. Two knives will be sufficient: a medium cook's knife and a small paring knife. Although they are much more difficult to sharpen, we prefer stainless steel knives. Carbon steel taints or blackens many foods, like avocados, eggplant, globe artichokes, red cabbage, and most fruit. Many people would also use a small serrated-edged knife, but this cannot be resharpened.

Lemon juicer. We have found that the traditional hand-held, carved wooden lemon juicer is the best and simplest tool for extracting small quantities of citrus juices.

Mixer. Whisking up mayonnaise in an electric mixer is very easy. If you do a lot of baking as well as salad making, a mixer with a grating/slicing attachment may be a better combination tool for you than a food processor.

Mortar and pestle. We hope you will buy your spices whole, that is, in their natural state. You will then need a mortar and pestle to pound and pulversize these seeds and pods. Buy a mortar with deep vertical sides to prevent the seeds from shooting out all over the kitchen.

Peeler. With a little practice the swivel-bladed vegetable peeler is quicker to use and less wasteful than our traditional fixed-blade potato peeler.

Pepper grinder. Absolutely essential; wherever we say "black pepper to taste," we mean freshly ground. Also useful for other spices, like coriander.

Scissors. Scissors are the best tool for trimming fresh herbs and for topping and tailing green beans and snow peas.

Other equipment. Other useful items not mentioned here would include colanders and sieves, a hand or rotary grater, measuring cups and spoons, mixing bowls, a salad spinner, a wire whisk, and wooden spoons.

Oils and Vinegars

Well-flavored oils and vinegars are essential for making attractive, tasty salads. They provide their own taste and are the base for any additional flavorings such as herbs or spices.

THE STRONGLY FLAVORED OILS

Olive oil. It is better to use a good olive oil with discretion than a poor one continuously. Good olive oil has a clean, fruity flavor, without any aftertaste. The lighter French and Italian olive oils are the most easily digested of all the cooking oils. The thick fruity oils from Greece and Spain are less easily digested. Try a bottle from each country in turn and discover, as you would with wines, which flavors and characteristics you prefer.

Even after you have decided which oil you prefer, you still have to decide on the grade. We would advise you to buy cold-pressed virgin oil. The best grades of this are Virgin Extra and Virgin Fine.

We would always use a good olive oil on leaf salads. You never use much vinaigrette, so the extra cost of using even the best olive oil as an ingredient is small. Although we have tried a wide range of olive oils in the restaurant, mayonnaise made from them has seldom been as well received as mayonnaise from the more neutral oils. This is our own experience, too, working with an even wider range of olive oils; but we must confess that we have had excellent olive oil-based mayonnaise in certain restaurants in France. Olive oil neither adds to nor reduces cholesterol levels in the blood.

Sesame oil. A sweet, nutty-flavored oil, very good in association with tamari or for cooking eggplant. Buy the thick, brownish, non-refined oil.

Walnut oil. An alternative to olive oil on the more robust green leaf salads, with a strong, nutty taste not to everyone's liking. Does not keep well; buy in small amounts and keep in a cool place.

THE NEUTRAL OILS

By definition, these are going to be generally quite similar, though different brands of the same oil may taste different. Some will be clean tasting; others will have a considerable aftertaste. Try several, and when you find the brand you like, stick to it.

Corn oil. The label may say it's good for salads, and several books may agree, but we have always found it heavy and flat. Keep it for frying.

Peanut oil. Much recommended by the prophets of the "new cuisine." Good varieties have a light, mild flavor, but unfortunately there seems to be a lot of inferior oil about.

Safflower oil. The ideal oil for anyone on a low-fat diet, it is very high in polyunsaturates.

Soy oil. We find this oil pleasant to use. Though it is often said to have a strong aftertaste, we have not found this so.

Sunflower oil. A thin, mild oil high in polyunsaturates. Add a little olive oil if you want more flavor.

VINEGARS

We could have suggested that you use rice vinegar in one recipe, sherry vinegar in another, wine vinegar in this and cider vinegar in that, but then your cupboards would soon be full of seldom-used bottles. So we have decided that an organically produced cider vinegar is the best all-around solution, and have used that in most recipes. It is more important that you have one good vinegar than a selection of inferior ones. This does not mean that you should only use one sort of vinegar—if you like a certain specialty vinegar, keep that as well. Avoid malt vinegar and distilled white vinegars.

You can produce your own flavored vinegars by infusing fresh herbs like marjoram, rosemary, tarragon, or thyme for at least a week in small bottles of vinegar.

Buying, Preparing, and Cooking Fresh Fruit and Vegetables

Apples. Our native fruit is of top quality. Apples are plentiful for much of the year, except for the period from late spring through midsummer, when we must settle for produce from controlled-atmosphere storage, or turn to imports from the southern hemisphere. Here are some suggestions for varieties at the peak of quality. Late summer: Paula Red, Tydeman Red, and Vistabella. Early autumn: McIntosh and Cortland (in the east), Jonathan (in the midwest). Late autumn: Red Delicious, Golden Delicious, Staymen/Winesap, and Northern Spy. Winter: Red Delicious. Late winter and early spring: Granny Smiths imported from New Zealand, Australia, Chile, and Argentina.

Artichokes, globe. Globe artichokes are in season from October to June, but are most plentiful and of the best quality in April and May. They should be green and crisp, without any withered leaves. Choose leafy, compact specimens, whose outer leaves are fleshy.

Soak the artichokes upside down for an hour in salted water to drive out any hidden insects. Pull or cut away, with a sharp stainless steel knife, any damaged outer leaves, and break off the stem. Rub cut surfaces with lemon juice. Immediately plunge each prepared artichoke into a bowl of acidulated water (2 tablespoons vinegar or lemon juice per quart).

When all the artichokes are prepared, swiftly drain them and drop them into rapidly boiling, salted and acidulated water in a stainless steel or enamel pan. Cook at a gentle boil for 20−35 minutes, accord-

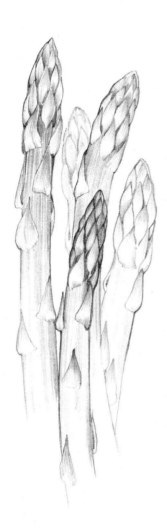

ing to their size. Pull off an outer leaf and test for tenderness. Stand them upside down to drain.

Asparagus. The short asparagus season runs from spring to early summer. Choose asparagus with tight heads, and, as freshness is all important, check that they have been recently cut by examining the severed stem. Generally, the thicker the shoots, the more expensive asparagus is. Of particularly good value are the long, thin stalks of asparagus, whose heads can be broken off just above their lower, stringy section. Thicker asparagus will need its coarse skin peeled off to expose the tender middle.

Tie the asparagus into individual serving-sized bundles and stand them, heads up, in a saucepan. Cook them in gently boiling, salted water for 5–15 minutes, according to the thickness of the stems. The heads themselves should steam above the level of the water. Take great care not to overcook.

Avocados. These were first brought to California when the Franciscan Fathers journeyed north from Mexico to establish the missions. The alligator-skinned California Haas avocados are recommended for their rich flavor and creamy texture. They are most plentiful from December to June. Florida avocados peak during the holiday season, from November to January. Like other fruit, avocados can only be enjoyed when properly ripe. They should be soft and give when touched, particularly around the neck. Buy avocados unripe and store them in a warm room until they reach this condition. The skins can be quite black before the flesh is overripe; however, the fruit with cracked, sunken, or badly bruised skins are usually beyond redemption. Use stainless steel knives to cut the flesh, and brush any stored avocado halves or pieces with lemon juice to retard the blackening process.

To halve avocados, make a deep encircling cut from the neck down to the base and back up to the neck. Give the avocado a sharp twist and lift away the free half. Still holding in the palm of your hand the avocado half with the stone embedded in it, lightly chop at the stone with your sharp knife so that the blade is held by the stone. Give the knife a sharp twist and the stone will come away on the knife blade.

To remove the avocado skin prior to slicing or dicing the flesh, lay the halves skin up on a chopping board and make several shallow cuts from the neck to the base. The skin can then be peeled off in segments.

Bean sprouts. Available all year round, these are very useful as a crisp, light component of winter salads. They can be bought in many supermarkets, but are exceptionally cheap if bought from a Chinese provision merchant. To prepare bean sprouts, just wash them and drain them thoroughly.

Beans, broad (Fava beans). These are not widely grown commercially in the United States, except in some of the southern states, where they are produced mainly for cattle feed. Home gardeners can try them. They do best in cool, humid weather, so plant them when you plant your peas. Pick them small and eat them raw, with just a scattering of sea salt, for a real treat.

Most store-bought broad beans are overmature and will need cooking. Use a minimum of lightly salted boiling water and cook until tender. If they are not tender after eight minutes, make a soup out of them.

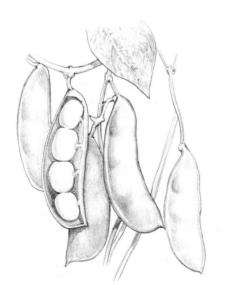

Beans, dried, chick-peas and lentils. All these legumes first need careful rinsing to remove stones and other foreign bodies. Dried beans absorb a great deal of water and will more than double their weight, so it is important to cover all the beans with enough water so they will still be submerged the following morning. Drain the beans, place them in a pan, and cover with fresh, *unsalted* water. Bring the beans to a boil, cook over a brisk heat for 5 minutes, cover, and reduce to a simmer. The beans will probably take nearly an hour to cook, but check them after half an hour and then every 10 minutes, adding a little water if necessary. Salt the beans just 5–10 minutes before you think they will be cooked. Drain but do not rinse the cooked beans.

Although it is not essential we think legumes are best cooked with flavorings like a carrot, half an onion, and a *bouquet garni* containing a sprig of thyme, a bay leaf, parsley stalks, and a celery stalk or lovage.

Beans, green. Bush and pole beans are the two main types, and new varieties are being tested in the marketplace every year. Slenderette bush beans give pencil-thin pods. Among pole beans, Kentucky Wonder is a perennial favorite for its flavor and productivity. The flat Romano Italian pole beans have a delicate, pleasing flavor.

Throughout summer local beans are cheap and plentiful. In winter the best come from Mexico and California. They are best eaten small. When you buy green beans, check that they are of equal size and maturity. If you grow your own, choose the smaller, smooth, even-sized, bright green pods.

Top and tail the beans and drop them into a pan of rapidly boiling salted water and cook, uncovered, over a brisk heat until barely tender (4–8 minutes). For use in salads, drain the beans immediately and plunge them into ice water or cool under cold running water.

Beets. Best when they are small, sweet and tender. In our southern states, they're grown as fall, winter and spring crops; in the middle states, they're harvested in early summer or late fall; and, in the north, as summer and early fall crops. Most plentiful from May to November, they can be found in markets year round.

Beets can be grated and eaten raw, but most people prefer them cooked. Cook them in boiling water; they are ready as soon as the skin will rub off— 15 to 45 minutes, depending on age and size. Never cut beets before cooking them. Just twist off the tops, or you will lose most of the color and flavor.

Broccoli. There are several types. Home-grown *sprouting broccoli* is not very common here, but it is occasionally available from roadside or farmers' markets, in both purple and white forms. The heads of this broccoli will open and expand without flowering. The season is very short and dependent on weather conditions. Sprouting broccoli is very tasty, with a strong flavor, but breaks up easily. It is excellent eaten on its own, like asparagus; don't toss it with other ingredients, or it will just turn to mush.

Most American-grown broccoli is of the green Italian kind called

Calabrese. It is in season year round, although July and August are low months. Most is grown in California and Texas. New York, New Jersey and Virginia also supply commercial markets. If you grow your own, remember that it does best in the cool weather of early summer and autumn.

Calabrese must be fresh. Only buy it when it has its distinctive bright green color. Avoid any heads that show signs of the yellowing flowers that are beginning to burst. In summer, it deteriorates quickly in the heat. If buying pre-packed broccoli, select bundles with stems of similar thickness so they will cook evenly.

To prepare broccoli, pull off any coarse leaves and trim the stalks, removing any tough parts (the stalks are as delicious as the flower heads) and peeling the skin back to the branches. Trim the stems if necessary to make them of even thickness; this way all parts will cook at the same rate.

Cook broccoli in 1 inch of very rapidly boiling salted water for 5–8 minutes until tender (squeeze the stalk to test). Gently drain the broccoli, and if it is to be served cold, chill it rapidly in iced water or under cold running water.

Cabbage. Red and white drumhead cabbages are available to us all year round, but between midspring and late summer they are expensive. Savoy cabbages are plentiful from late autumn to early spring.

When preparing cabbages, cut away the coarse ribs and the central core. Try to cut the cabbage into thin strips in such a way that its wavy corrugated leaves are seen to full advantage.

Carrots. Even in the North, fresh, home-grown carrots are available for much of the year. Delicate thinnings can be eaten in early spring, and part of the mature crop can be held in the ground through winter if heavily mulched, actually improving in flavor in this natural cold storage.

The sweetest commercial carrots come to us from California year round. Texas, Florida, Arizona, and Canada are also big producers.

Early spring finger carrots can be simply brushed clean. Later on in

the season they need peeling; otherwise, the skin darkens and looks unappetizing.

Cauliflower. Most cauliflower is grown in New York, Texas, Florida, California, and Washington. Northern crops peak from late summer through early fall and then the western and southern crops take over until early spring. Like many vegetables, cauliflower is expensive in early spring. Outside that period their price varies enormously, since storage is a problem. Once cauliflower is ready for picking it doesn't keep well on the plant, nor does it keep well once cut. The result is that sometimes the wholesale markets have too much cauliflower and it is cheap, and sometimes they don't have enough to go around and it is expensive. The moral of the story is buy cauliflower when it is cheap and ignore it when it is expensive. A cauliflower's face is its fortune: if it looks good it will taste good. Choose heavy, white, unpitted heads.

Experiment using cauliflower raw; it has a wonderful crunchy texture. Never use over-cooked cauliflower in salads. It is best steamed or parboiled in 1–2 inches of lightly salted boiling water. The florets will be cooked in 5 minutes, while the whole heads will take a little more than 15 minutes. Chill the cooked cauliflower in the usual manner to prevent it from going mushy.

Celeriac. Also known as bulb or root celery, celeriac is much neglected in this country—a great pity, for it has a fine flavor. Start looking for it in early autumn. It looks like a small rutabaga with a wrinkled skin. Celeriac for salads, diced, sliced, or cut in julienne, is often blanched by dropping it in boiling water for one minute. Drain the celeriac well before dressing. Choose regular-looking roots, heavy for their size; they should not have too many deep crevices or bulbous swellings. Avoid any celeriac with soft brown patches.

Once celeriac has been peeled and cut, it must be immediately placed in acidulated water (2 tablespoons vinegar per quart), or it will have discolored before you have a chance to put the dressing on.

Celery. Available to us the whole year round, but most plentiful and cheapest from October to April. California and Florida are the largest producers of the green Pascal varieties. A few home gardeners may still blanch their celery.

Avoid putting more than a few celery leaves in a salad; they are just too bitter.

Corn, sweet. We confess that we have used canned sweet corn for most of the recipes in this book. We do use fresh corn from mid- to late summer when ears of local sweet corn can be bought cheaply. It must be very fresh since, once cut, sweet corn rapidly loses its flavor.

Choose bright green husks with dark brown silks and plump creamy yellow kernels. (It will not matter if the kernels at the top are not yet mature.) Husk the corn and drop it into a pan of rapidly boiling, *unsalted* water. The corn will be cooked 2–3 minutes after the water has returned to the boil. For use in salads, cool the ears, hold them vertically on a chopping board, and cut off the kernels with a sharp knife.

Cucumbers. Available all year round, these are at their best and cheapest during the hotter months. If they are expensive, use alternate salad ingredients. Choose firm, dark green fruit, and avoid any that are large or bloated. Whether you peel cucumbers or leave them intact is usually a matter of personal taste. It is, however, a good idea to reduce the water content in cucumbers by placing the sliced or diced fruit in a colander, sprinkling it with salt, and leaving it lightly pressed to drain for at least half an hour. The cucumber need not be rinsed after this operation as the salt will drain away with the water (you will probably not need to resalt the salad). The water content can be further reduced by cutting the whole fruit in half lengthwise and removing the watery seeds by running the back of a teaspoon firmly along the seed channel. Slice the cucumber, and salt as described.

Eggplants. Though available most of the year, we believe eggplants have most flavor when grown in warmer regions where they can prosper without too much artificial feeding and protection. Choose glossy, firm, unblemished specimens with good fresh stems. Reject any eggplants without stems because the retailer may have removed the

stems when they began to wither or go moldy. Size has little effect on eggplant's flavor. If possible, always use plastic, stainless steel, or enamel utensils when preparing and cooking eggplants, as they blacken on contact with carbon steel or aluminum.

Eggplants may be sliced and salted and left lightly pressed to drain in a colander for 30 minutes or more to draw off some of their slightly bitter juices. This also reduces the amount of oil they absorb while being fried.

Fennel. Bulb or Italian fennel is at its best in summer, but it is often overlooked because there is such a choice of vegetables at that time. Local bulb fennel is available in late summer and early autumn. Fennel remains available throughout autumn and winter, and although it makes a refreshing change during the latter part of the year, its quality progressively diminishes. Choose firm, unwithered bulbs free of blemishes.

Prepare the fennel for salads by removing any tough lower stalks or outer skins and cutting out the solid center core. Slice the prepared bulb as desired.

Garlic. This is available throughout the year, with the supply lowest in the fall. California and Arizona are the biggest suppliers. Take great care when frying garlic because it burns very quickly.

Grapefruit. Late autumn through early spring is the season for high-quality grapefruit from Florida and Texas. Thick-skinned California grapefruit are available from April to October, but they're expensive and of lesser quality, especially in the summer.

Leaf vegetables. See page 24.

Leeks. In late spring and early summer look for the delicious, tiny, finger-thick leeks. In late autumn, winter, and early spring, the white and very pale green parts of mature leeks, sliced very finely, can be used in many salads to replace onions.

To prepare tiny leeks, cut off the roots, trim back the green tops, and remove any damaged outer layers. Make a deep vertical cut down through the green top into the white section and wash the leaves thoroughly under the tap to remove any soil. Prepare mature leeks for salads by cutting off the roots and green tops and finely slicing the white stem into rounds. Place the rounds in a colander, press them out into rings and wash well.

Lemons. They come from the same regions as oranges. Though available all year round, they are more expensive outside the main autumn and winter season.

Limes. Florida and California grow most of our limes. Available all year round at a fairly constant price, in late summer they are often cheaper than lemons. Some are very sharp.

Mushrooms. Available throughout the year, they're not a seasonal vegetable because they are grown in caves or windowless hothouses with controlled temperature and humidity. Only the fresh, closed, white button mushrooms should be used in salads. They can be served raw, finely sliced and dressed with lemon juice or an herb-flavored vinaigrette.

Onions, spring onions, and shallots. While mature onions are obviously available all the year round, they reach us from many parts of the country and the world and exhibit very different characteristics. Always taste a small piece of the onion before deciding how much to put in a salad. If it tastes extremely harsh, reduce the quantity used or replace it with a milder spring onion or shallot. We do recommend the sweet midsummer Spanish onion for salads, and especially the very sweet Vidalia onions that come from Georgia in June and July.

Spring onions are used freely in Creole and oriental cooking. Try finely sliced larger spring onions in salads.

In late summer and early autumn when the new-season shallots are first available they may seem very expensive, but try asking your grocer for a small net of them. Hang this in a dry airy place, and use the delicately flavored, aromatic bulbs all winter and on into early spring.

Oranges. These are cheapest from November through May. The large, thin-skinned Florida and Texas navel oranges are in season in November and December. Thick-skinned California navels are in the markets from December through May. Florida and Texas Valencias are available through the winter and spring. In summer, Valencias from California are in season.

Pears. These like slightly warmer conditions than apples. The season begins and ends with California pears: the Bartletts in midsummer and Anjous as late as spring. Look for Bartletts and Russets from local growers at roadside stands and in food markets in late summer and early autumn. Bosc and Seckel pears come soon after them. The natural season is extended by retarding ripening in cool storage, which causes loss of flavor.

Peas, green. Unless you grow them yourself, fresh garden peas are a thing of the past. You can buy peas in the pod, but in our experience they will contain as many coarse, overripe, starch-laden peas as young fresh green peas.

Peas, snap (sugar snap). This is the tastiest of all recent vegetable introductions. The whole pod is eaten, and the peas are prepared and cooked in the same way as green beans (page 13). Try growing snap peas yourself.

Peas, snow. These are delicious, bringing the freshness of early summer to our dark winter and early spring days. The best ones are imported from Mexico. They are always expensive. Take care when you buy snow peas because far too many on sale are grossly overmature. The pods must be quite flat, the tiny peas registering no more than a dot in their bright green overcoats. If this is not the case, you are buying disappointment.

Prepare the pods by snapping off the stalk and pulling it backwards towards the tip to remove the coarse thread. Cook as for green beans (page 13).

Peppers, sweet. Available all the year round from a variety of sources. Peppers are at their cheapest from midsummer to midautumn. Red peppers are always more expensive than green peppers. The less common yellow and black fruit taste and cost much the same as the red peppers.

To prepare raw peppers, remove the stem and seed cluster and remove loose seeds. For a richer, sweeter flavor and a soft texture, remove the skin from the peppers by baking them in a very hot oven for 15–20 minutes or placing them under a hot grill or on a fork over a naked gas flame, turning the peppers as each side blackens and blisters. Rinse off the blistered skin under the cold tap and pat dry.

Peppers, hot (chilies). There are nearly 100 types of hot chili peppers in use in Mexico, three, four, or more different ones being used in the preparation of just one dish. California and Florida produce several varieties, from the mild Long Green-Anaheim, Yellow-Caribe, and Banana peppers to the hottest green Serrano. Like sweet peppers, chilies are at their cheapest from midsummer to midautumn, from local growers. The best and easiest to use is the jalapeño pepper. They are very hot, so you only need buy them in small quantities. Add less than the recommended amount of chilies until you discover how hot they are.

To prepare chili peppers, cut off the stalks, slit the bodies of the peppers open, remove and discard the seeds (although in Mexico they would not be wasted). Do not rub your eyes or face and wash your hands immediately after you have finished handling them.

Pineapples. Hawaiian pineapples are the largest, juiciest, and sweetest. They arrive almost ripe and are most plentiful from late autumn through the winter and early spring. Pineapples from South America and the Caribbean are available year round. In salads, canned fruit is a poor substitute for the real thing.

Pomegranates. A fun fruit available only in autumn, from California. The beautiful red, bitter-sweet seeds are more than just a garnish when added to crisp leaf or fruit salads.

Potatoes. If you buy seed stock from a specialized garden store, you can grow your own red salad potatoes (such as Chieftain, Red Pontiac, and Early Rose). Unfortunately, the consumer in American food markets can't select potatoes by named variety. Florida red potatoes are in season from autumn through spring. There are some firm-fleshed white potatoes that are also quite good in salads. Grow your own or ask your produce manager for Katahdin (in the Northeast), Sebago (in the Southeast), or Centennial (in the West).

If you are prepared to pay, you can have new potatoes from Florida in late winter. Their season moves north and west and ends in June, just when, in the North, local ones begin to come in with the first peas.

New potatoes should just be washed and brushed clean. Trim off any green or damaged areas. Clean and trim older potatoes in a similar manner. Cook potatoes in boiling salted water, in their skins. For salads, remove the skins while the potatoes are still warm (sometimes they will just pull off). Remember to cut large potatoes into easy-to-eat pieces before you pour on the dressing.

Radishes. Radishes are at their best in late spring and early summer when, with the soil and the sun getting warmer every day, they grow fast and furiously, producing succulent, crisp, peppery roots. Once the summer sun has dried out the ground, the roots are most tender. We think it is better to use the large white radish (also called daikon) from late summer onwards. When buying our traditional red radish, look for firm, bright unblemished roots with good fresh dark green leaves still attached. Avoid oversized roots; they will be hollow and bitter fleshed. When choosing daikon, pick roots about 1 inch thick.

Tomatoes. Trying to buy tasty tomatoes is a bit like trying to follow a treasure trail. Here are some clues to help you towards the goal.

In cold seasons, buy tomatoes from the warmer, sunnier growing areas, since tomatoes prosper in the sun. In high season, buy local tomatoes that have not yet lost the smell of the tomato plant. Nothing can equal the flavor and texture of a sun-ripened tomato from the home garden or a local grower. In late fall and early winter, Florida and California supply two-thirds of the tomatoes to our commercial markets. Mexican imports are the best choice in winter.

Whatever the season, look out for the high-flavored varieties such as the tiny, dark red Sweet 100 cherry tomatoes, Roma plum tomatoes, early Springset and Jet Star, mid-season Big Boy and Better Boy, and the large, meaty, late Beefsteaks. Sadly, plant breeders of commercially grown varieties seem more concerned with the genes that produce even-sized fruit than with the genes that produce the flavor.

To skin tomatoes, bring a medium-sized pan of water to a boil. Take the tomatoes, and with a sharp pointed knife, remove the stalk and that hard little section of flesh to which the stalk is attached. Drop the tomatoes, one or two at a time, into the boiling water for several seconds. Remove them with a slotted spoon and cool them under cold water. The tomato skin will easily peel or even fall off. Remove excess liquid and seeds from tomatoes by cutting them in half horizontally and gently squeezing and shaking out the liquid.

Zucchini. Throughout summer local zucchini are cheap and plentiful. In winter the best ones come from Mexico and California. Choose zucchini no more than six inches in length, with tight, unblemished skins. The yellow variety looks tremendous in salads.

Cook zucchini whole in boiling, salted water for 5 minutes or until they give just a little when gently squeezed. Rapidly chill them, top and tail, and slice into $\frac{3}{8}$-inch sections. To fry zucchini, cut in a similar manner, place in a colander, sprinkle with salt, and leave, lightly pressed, to drain for an hour. Rinse and dry the slices before frying them. Zucchini can also be sliced wafer-thin and served raw, although we usually steam them for 2 minutes to make them more digestible.

LEAF VEGETABLES

If you want a green leaf salad or just a light crisp salad in winter or early spring, there are plenty of alternatives, but you may have to pay a little extra. Into your cold season salad bowl goes Romaine or iceberg lettuce, the chicories and endives, Chinese cabbage, bean sprouts, dandelion leaves, newly sprouted sorrel, spinach, and watercress.

While it is fairly obvious when these leaf vegetables are in good condition, remember the following points:

- Clean, neat lettuces in little polythene bags will almost certainly be less tasty than the big, untrimmed specimens with soil still on their outer leaves.

- Check, particularly with Romaine lettuce, that they have not begun to bolt. If they have, the leaves will be bitter, not sweet.
- Variety is very important in leaf salads. Buy several sorts to use together and keep them wrapped in damp newspapers in the bottom of the refrigerator.

PREPARING LEAF VEGETABLES

1. Nearly all the leaf vegetables are very fragile. Handle them with care when stripping the plants down, washing and drying the leaves, and tossing the completed salad.
2. Drain and shake the leaves dry. Don't serve salads with a puddle underneath them. If you don't have a salad spinner, use the old-fashioned method—place the washed leaves in a large, clean dishtowel, hold the four corners, and swing the dishtowel in a lazy circle outside the back door.
3. It is unnecessary, indeed detrimental, to wash the extremely tightly packed hearts of Belgian endive, iceberg lettuce, Chinese cabbage, and some varieties of Romaine lettuce.
4. Unless you are going to use the leaf salad immediately, gently tear (don't cut) the leaves into smaller pieces. If you do cut the leaves, you will find that they bleed and collapse in a very short time. Moreover, cut leaves have a uniformity of shape we are seeking to avoid. Heavy, ribbed leaves such as Romaine lettuce can be cut along the rib without ill effect.

DRESSING LEAF SALADS

1. It is worth reserving your very best olive oil for your leaf salads. Chicory (curly endive) and dandelion are best dressed with walnut oil, but use it on other leaf salads as well if you like its flavor. Make your dressing with a 4/1, or if you are just using delicate leaves, a 5/1 oil/vinegar ratio.
2. Never dress your leaf salads until the very last moment, preferably at the table.
3. Toss your salad gently but thoroughly, scooping the leaves from the bottom of the heap to the top several times over.

LEAF VEGETABLES
FOR SALADS

Bok choy (Pak choi or Chinese chard). Available in markets year round, it grows best in cool weather. Buy the smallest available, separate the leaves, wash well, dry, and slice into small pieces.

Belgian endive (Witloof chicory). The pale green and white "teeth" (*chicons*) of imported Belgian endive make a very pleasant addition to our autumn, winter, and early spring salads. This is a good salad standby as it keeps well if wrapped in plastic film and placed in the refrigerator. Choose endive with tight, pointed leaves and no brown blemishes. The inner leaves are so closely packed that it is unnecessary to wash them. Belgian endive is less bitter than its cousin, chicory (curly endive).

Bibb and Boston lettuce. A favorite for home gardens, it grows best in cool weather. Florida and California supply much to commercial markets. The small, round heads have thick, succulent midribs. Use if you like a softer lettuce.

Chicory (Curly endive). Hot weather makes it too bitter, so its season is fall to early spring. Chicory looks like a riotous mop of ragged-edged leaves. Make sure when you buy that none of the leaves are slimy. It has a very bitter but refreshing taste. Serve in small quantities.

Chinese cabbage. Available throughout the cold months from Florida and California, although there is some locally grown Chinese cabbage also on the market in early summer and early autumn. This vegetable has much improved in quality over the last few years and the long, narrow variety is superior to the short, chunky type. When buying, check just inside the tip for brown rot. Remove any damaged outer leaves.

Cress (Peppergrass). The pungent flavor of the tightly curled leaves are a nice addition to salads. Easy to grow in the home garden or on a sunny windowsill.

Dandelion. This should be picked in early spring before it flowers. It can be very bitter, so use in small quantities.

Escarole. Peak season for escarole is winter and spring, although it is available year round. It looks like a slightly ragged lettuce. Prepare it as for lettuce; because of its bitter flavor it is best mixed with other greens.

Iceberg lettuce. California, New York and New Jersey give us most of the iceberg lettuce in summer and fall. In winter and early spring, it comes from Florida and Arizona. Iceberg lettuce has a fine, crisp texture, but little flavor. Mix it with contrasting darker, tastier leaves. The hearts of this variety are so tightly packed it is best to cut them in half before pulling them apart.

Lambs' lettuce (corn salad). With delicious, dark green leaves the size and shape of a lambs' tongue, this can be grown in cool weather in the home garden, or it may be found in a specialty produce market. It tends to be expensive, but is well worthwhile for a special occasion.

Looseleaf lettuce. Fragile leaves add delicacy to a light salad. Home gardeners can choose from green, ruby, and oak leaf varieties.

Mustard greens. These have a powerful, fiery taste and are easily home grown.

Radicchio. A round, beautiful deep red endive with a white contrasting rib, sometimes available from specialty produce markets. It looks rather like a large red Brussels sprout. Since it is imported from Italy, it is never cheap. It has quite a bitter taste. Buy just one head for its aesthetic value.

Romaine (Cos) lettuce. Available year round, from local producers and Canada in the warm months, and from California, Arizona, and Florida in cold weather. Combines crisp texture with mild, sweet flavor.

Sorrel. See Summer Green Salad (page 57).

Spinach and beet greens. In spring, use the pale green immature leaves from the newly sprouting plants.

Watercress. This is available at all times of the year, from Florida in winter and from local growers in the north in spring and summer.

To prepare watercress for use, trim away the roots and wash thoroughly. Store, damp, in a sealed plastic container in the salad drawer of the refrigerator.

Pantry Essentials

Few modern households have enough space for storing vast supplies of foodstuffs, and for those that do there is always the danger that many ingredients will go to waste or grow stale before they are used. Our tip is to keep a small storage cupboard of the best ingredients available, augment it with some personal favorites, and extend its range by exploring one foreign cuisine at a time. If you find you dislike certain foreign foods, disregard them and their ingredients. You will probably never get to like them. Give any unwanted ingredients away at once or dispose of them since you do not want to have never-to-be-used materials cluttering up your kitchen. Kitchens are workshops and should be kept clear.

This is our selection of pantry staples. Those items in *italics* we consider essential; the others are desirable but up to personal taste.

Spices. *Black pepper, coriander, cumin, paprika,* cayenne, sea salt, juniper, caraway, mustard seeds, white pepper, curry powder. See also pages 32 to 33.

Flavorings. *Tamari, sesame paste (tahini), hot pepper sauce, garlic,* shallots, fresh ginger root, mango chutney, peanut butter, coconut butter.

Oils. *Olive oil, a neutral oil* (peanut or sunflower), walnut oil, sesame oil.

Vinegars. *Organic cider vinegar,* rice wine vinegar, red wine vinegar.

Herbs. Grow as many fresh salad herbs as you can. We think only oregano and, perhaps, dill and mint are worth storing dried.

Canned goods. *Plum tomatoes,* sweet corn.

Bottled or preserved goods. *Olives,* pickled gherkins, horseradish sauce, *Dijon mustard.*

Grains, beans and legumes. *Red kidney beans, white beans, chick-peas,* large brown or green lentils, navy beans, bulgur wheat.

Dried pasta. Keep one box of the short elbow, shell, or twist shapes. A similar green pasta is attractive but not essential.

Nuts. None are essential, but walnuts and almonds and (to a lesser degree) hazelnuts are all useful.

Seeds. Again, none are essential, but both blue poppy seeds and the buff-colored sesame seeds are very useful. Toasted sunflower seeds are a pleasant, nutritious addition to many salads.

Luxuries. Totally subjective, but ours would be cardamom seeds, pine nuts, pesto, pistachio nuts, tamarind seeds, limes in season.

Short-term storage. The following are extremely handy to have in your refrigerator: natural yogurt, whipping cream, sour cream, fresh bean curd (tofu), fresh coconut, lemons.

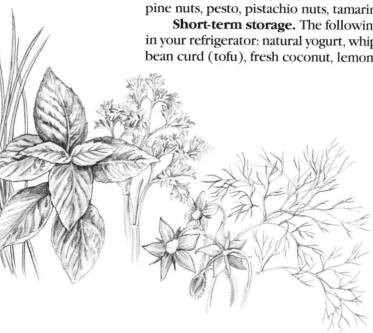

Herbs, Spices, and Other Flavorings for Salads

HERBS

Robust herbs such as bay, thyme, and rosemary retain some of their original flavor even when dried. This flavor can be leached out to other foods in slow cooking processes. When it comes to salad making, however, there are no such processes, and the herbs used here should, where possible, be fresh, ready, and eager to bestow their flavor and bouquet upon the ingredients with which they associate. The best salad herbs are extremely delicate, and once dried, taste and smell like slightly moldy dried grass rather than their true selves.

You only need a window ledge to grow most herbs. A few fresh herbs will bring individuality and distinction to the most mundane salad.

To flavor salads with dried herbs, beat them well into the dressing shortly before you pour it over the salad. Never sprinkle them across the top of a completed salad since they cannot transmit their flavor to the salads by just sitting there, and, in fact, are more likely to stick in your throat.

Basil. If you are going to grow just one herb, this should be it. Germinate the seeds in a warm space in midspring and set the plants in a sunny spot outdoors after all danger of frost is past. Established basil plants can also sometimes be bought from nurserymen in late spring and early summer. The large-leaved sweet basil is much superior to the peppery, tiny-leaved bush basil, but the latter is slightly hardier and sprigs of its leaves make an interesting addition to green salads. At the end of the growing season, basil leaves can be preserved under good olive oil.

The sweet fragrant flavor of basil is superb with tomatoes and sweet peppers. Its fragrance is soon lost and it is best added to salads just before serving. Basil leaves should be torn, not chopped.

Chervil. A small, delicate, feathery-leaved plant, best grown in light shade to keep the plants from running to seed. Sow outdoors in succession from early spring onwards.

Chervil has a mild licorice flavor and is excellent in cream dressings, with eggs, and as a constituent with parsley, chives, and tarragon in the traditional French mixture, *fines herbes.* Like basil, its flavor is soon lost, and it is best added to the dressing or salad just prior to serving.

Chives. Buy the plants in spring. If they are to be kept in a pot they must be kept well fed and watered. Keep several plants and keep them well trimmed back with scissors.

Chives, like chervil, go well with all dairy products. They have a delicate flavor and though they look attractive on a potato salad they really have not got the character to liven up bland potatoes on their own. Their pretty lavender flowers can look very decorative.

Cilantro (coriander). Fresh green cilantro (or Chinese parsley) is very popular in the Middle East and is obtainable in this country from Indian and Middle-Eastern stores or from specialty produce markets. Cilantro is also quite easy to grow.

Cilantro leaf has an odor of cats; nothing so aptly describes it. This smell gives no clue to the excellent flavor, which brings a subtle taste to many dishes.

Dill. A favorite herb throughout much of northern Europe, buckets and buckets of dill can be seen in flower-like bouquets in markets in Copenhagen and Stockholm. Look for it at farmers' markets and in specialty produce markets.

Dill can be easily grown. Sow in succession from early spring onwards, as it rapidly turns to seed. We think it is an herb well worth cultivating, though it will not grow properly in pots.

Try dill with potatoes, cucumbers, cream, tomato soups, and oily fish. Dried dill does retain much of the herb's natural flavor, but of course it entirely lacks the visual appeal of the delicate, feathery, fresh leaf.

Fennel. An extremely attractive plant from early spring till autumn and well worth growing for its appearance alone. It is easy to grow in any reasonably sunny position. In mild districts, new growth appears as soon as the old has died back, and a mature plant will grow over six feet high. Fennel can be grown in pots, but it will not thrive.

All parts of the plant have culinary uses. Chop the abundant, anise-flavored leaves and use freely with grated carrot and more sparingly over cauliflower, cucumber, green beans, and salad potatoes. Branches of young fennel leaves make particularly attractive garnishes as they have a high resistance to wilting.

Hyssop. Another attractive, easy-to-grow herb which will thrive in pots, this evergreen perennial can grow to a height of twenty inches.

Hyssop is just the herb to make a green leaf salad special. Its flavor is bitter, predominantly of mint but with many subtle underflavors. Take care; this flavor is strong. Choose only the young, tender leaves and use them sparingly, or for a more delicate flavor use just the tiny, bright blue flowers.

Marjoram. This has a mild, pleasant flavor. It is half hardy and grows to about 12 inches. You can keep a winter supply by potting plants in late summer and keeping them indoors.

Mint. There are innumerable varieties of mint. The two best for culinary uses are the common spearmint and the round-leaved apple mint. If you wish to grow only one type, it is safer to grow the apple mint, as it is resistant to the rust disease frequently fatal to spearmint. Mint grows very easily in damp, sunny, or semi-shaded positions. It is a good idea to confine the plants in sunken, bottomless buckets or flue tiles to prevent the underground runners from strangling less robust plants.

Mint is used extensively in Middle-Eastern cooking, and it appears in a number of recipes in this book.

Oregano or wild marjoram. To our knowledge, oregano is the only herb that is better dried than fresh. Use oregano as an alternative to fresh basil. In southern Italy, the two are often used together over tomato salads.

Parsley. The only problem with growing parsley is that the seeds take a long time to germinate. A continuous supply of this herb can be arranged by covering parsley growing in open ground with cloches or by bringing pot-grown parsley indoors to a light position. Flat-leaved or continental parsley, as it is called in the shops, invariably has more flavor than the curly-leaved varieties. Look for big bunches of this flat-leaved type in Greek or Indian food shops, particularly in winter and spring when your local market may have ceased to stock the herb.

When parsley is plentiful and cheap use it lavishly. Far too often, people thoughtlessly scatter it in tiny amounts over every dish. It is far better to consider carefully which dishes it best complements and to use it heavily on those alone. Dried parsley detracts from any dish to which it is added.

Tarragon. French tarragon should sue the common Russian tarragon for defamation of character. It is quite a different plant, and growing the Russian variety is a waste of time and space. French tarragon seldom sets seeds, and therefore packets of seeds marked tarragon are invariably the worthless Russian type. You will have to buy plants of French tarragon. It is a semi-hardy perennial that will need some protection in severe weather. It dies right back to the ground in late autumn. To keep healthy plants, it is necessary to repropagate every second or third year by careful division of the root stocks or, better still, by tip cuttings. Tarragon does best in a sunny position in moist, rich soil. It will grow in pots if they are large enough. Although it is one of the "grande" culinary herbs, its use in salads is usually confined to flavoring green salads, or in conjunction with chervil, parsley, and chives in *fines herbes* dressings. It has a great affinity with fish and chicken dishes and is delicious in mayonnaise.

Thyme. Not really a salad herb but such a cheerful little plant, which grows so easily on a window ledge or in a barren little patch of earth, that it would be a pity not to encourage it.

Thyme is probably the most extensively used culinary herb. Fresh thyme is wonderful, and thyme plucked in young flower and dried and kept on its little branches seems to keep its sweet fragrance. Dried thyme in bottles or packets, however, brings a musty, acrid taste to any casserole to which it is added.

SPICES

Try to buy and keep all spices in their natural state, as pods and seeds, since few packages and wrappings will protect the potency of the spice as well as Nature does. Vacuum packing is fine until you have to break the seal; seldom do you use all the ground spice immediately and ground spices rapidly lose their flavor. You will, of course, need a mortar and pestle (or a coffee grinder) to grind the pods and seeds to powder. It you do need to purchase pre-ground spices, buy them in small quantities.

Many Indian shops sell spices very cheaply, and their regular customers demand good quality and ensure a rapid turnover. It is better and cheaper to buy your spices from these shops, and to replace old stock with new at regular intervals, than to pay dearly for brand-name packaging in supermarkets.

Keep spices out of the light in air-tight jars. Many seeds are best lightly dry-roasted or toasted in a heavy, cast-iron pan prior to grinding. This really brings out the flavor, especially with cumin and coriander seeds.

Caraway. These seeds are small, dark, curved, and pungent. They are used extensively in Austrian and Hungarian cooking, frequently in association with paprika. The flavor is very strong and not everyone's favorite. Use caraway seeds with discretion in cabbage salads.

Coriander. This spice can be grown for its seeds in this country, but since they are very cheap to buy, it is seldom worth the effort to cultivate it. If you do grow coriander, the seeds must not be picked until they are fully ripe or else their flavor is unpleasant.

The small, ball-like seeds crush easily and have a mild, sweet, citrus flavor. Coriander combines well with lemon flavors and is used in almost all the world's cuisines.

Cumin. The common seasoning in Mexican and Middle-Eastern cooking. Its seeds visually resemble caraway but are paler, less curved, and have a very different flavor. Indeed, cumin freshly toasted and ground is one of the finest smells ever to come from a kitchen.

Ground cumin does wonders for bean salads. It is also very good with low-fat dairy products such as yogurt and cottage cheese and is a major constituent in those delicious Middle-Eastern nut and spice dressings.

Juniper. The small blue-black berries have much more flavor than the reddish-brown ones. They should be crushed before use. Juniper brings a pleasant flavor to red cabbage salads.

Mustard. If you use powdered English mustard, you must add cold water to it and let it stand for at least 10 minutes to let the characteristic flavor develop. If you do not, or if you add hot water or vinegar, you will get a milder, bitter taste which we do not like but which agrees with some people.

We generally prefer to use the slightly softer Dijon or the milder English mustards to give bite to vinaigrette or cream dressings. You can achieve quite a different, sweet flavor from mustard seeds by popping them in a small quantity of very hot oil in a small saucepan. Pour the mustard seeds and oil out of the hot saucepan as soon as the seeds have popped, or else they will carbonize and spoil. The seeds and flavored oil are very good over carrots and other young vegetables.

Pepper. When we say "season with pepper," we invariably mean freshly ground black pepper. Occasionally, we will use freshly ground white pepper, when in, say, a pale mayonnaise, we may not want black flecks to show up. We may use *cayenne pepper*, which is powdered hot red chilies, when we need a hotter, less aromatic taste. *Paprika pepper,* derived from ripe red bell peppers that are dried and ground, is mild and sweet and goes well with many vegetables and dairy products. We find that the best paprika is bright red, not orange. It is worthwhile noting and sticking to a good supply as many paprikas have a harsh, sawdust-like taste. Hungarian paprika seems to be the most reliable.

OTHER FLAVORS

Fresh ginger root. This is very reasonably priced and obtainable in many supermarkets, as well as most Middle-Eastern, Chinese, and Indian shops. Try to select smooth-skinned young rhizomes. Peel and hand-grate the ginger and mix the shreds with chopped spring onions, shallots, chilies, and tamari, or sesame oil. Use over bean sprouts, cucumber, or tender young vegetables.

Hot pepper sauce. Hot pepper sauce is a useful alternative to fresh chilies. It has a smoother taste than cayenne pepper, and it is easier to adjust the heat of a dressing with it than with chili powder. Hot pepper sauce comes in many styles with all sorts of additions, but we prefer the simple Singapore-style sauce complete with seeds, available in most Chinese groceries.

Tamari (soy sauce). We think the natural tamari, generally Japanese in origin and obtainable from health food shops, is greatly superior to the soy sauce on sale in supermarkets and produce markets. Tamari has a rounder, fuller, more mellow flavor than ordinary soy sauce, which is chemically produced and often has a harsh, slightly metallic taste. We use the paler varieties of tamari, as they do not spoil the colors of bright salad vegetables.

Tahini (sesame paste). This thick, peanut-butter-like paste made from crushed sesame seeds is a delicious and nutritious flavoring. Thin it down with water, yogurt, and lemon juice and add other flavors to make many tasty dips and dressings.

NOTE

**Unless otherwise specified, all the recipes
in this book are for 4 people.**

Spring Salads

Spring is not the easiest season in which to find a wide variety of good salad ingredients, so now is the time to exercise most discrimination and to make full use of the pantry. Winter vegetables that have been put away by the farmers and wholesalers are getting a little tired, fruit is losing its crispness, and the local farmer is mainly sowing and planting rather than harvesting. All is not lost, however, since spring starts earlier in the southern states and we can rely on their produce to add variety to the homegrown fruit and vegetables. Again, care is needed in buying, since some produce travels better than others and some fruits and vegetables can be very costly.

SPRING FRUITS AND VEGETABLES

The vegetables at their best at this time and the ones we most recommend for spring salads are radishes, new potatoes, little white turnips, asparagus, spinach, beet greens, and watercress. Also make good use of mushrooms, zucchini, and bean sprouts. Worthwhile imports from warmer regions are snow peas, green beans, tomatoes, Belgian endive, broccoli, chicory, globe artichokes, and cucumbers. Parsley and particularly mint are readily available fresh herbs and are useful for garnishes and dressings. Of the fruits available, all citrus fruits, plus pineapples, strawberries, bananas, and avocados are the best buys.

Radishes Served with Aperitifs or as an Appetizer

3–4 radishes per person

This recipe is the simplest one in the book, and that is its virtue. The bright red roots and fresh green leaves of the radishes are arranged on a plain white plate, or cascade over ice cubes in a glass bowl set on a sparkling white tablecloth. Any good quality radish can be used, but the variety French Breakfast, with their white tips, look best of all when served in this way.

Buy the very best-looking radishes you can find. Wash them well, putting aside any that are marked or misshapen. Now cut off the tap root only and remove the first two leaves (the seedling leaves). Place the radishes in the refrigerator and leave them for at least one hour before serving.

The clean, crisp, slightly peppery taste of the radishes makes them excellent partners to nearly all the traditional aperitifs or cocktails.

Alternatively, serve the radishes with fresh brown bread, butter, and sea salt as a very simple but effective first course.

Fennel and Grapefruit Salad

1 pound bulb fennel, washed and trimmed
2 grapefruits, peel and pith cut away
2 tablespoons olive oil
½ teaspoon salt
fennel leaves for garnish

It is often the simplest combination that works best, and so it is with this salad. The sharp, juicy grapefruit is a perfect partner for the crunchy, anise-flavored fennel.

Cut away and discard the hard cores of the fennel bulbs. Slice the bulbs into thin sections and place these in a bowl. Cut the grapefruit into slices and pull these apart over the bowl, letting the chunks fall over the fennel. Discard any skin or other indigestible matter that is easily removed. Add the olive oil and salt and mix thoroughly. Turn into a serving dish and garnish with fennel leaves.

1½−2 pounds small new potatoes
salt to taste
2−3 sprigs fresh mint
5 fluid ounces Vinaigrette
    Dressing (page 125)
1 heaped tablespoon fresh,
    finely chopped parsley

Around the time the first shoots of mint are braving the spring weather, the availability of little brown, pebblelike new potatoes is much improved. They can be found from Christmas onward, though the earlier you buy them the more they will cost. These very small potatoes have a wonderful earthy taste which we like to complement with a simple tangy dressing.

Wash the potatoes clean under a running tap. Do not scrub or peel them, just cut out any damaged areas. Drop them into a pan of boiling salted water and cook on medium heat for 20 minutes or more. Sometimes these potatoes are very dense and take a surprisingly long time to cook. Test new potatoes by lifting one of the larger ones out with a wooden spoon and giving it a gentle squeeze. If it gives a little, it's cooked. Drain potatoes and set aside in a serving bowl to cool.

Mix together the mint, vinaigrette, and parsley, and then pour over the cooled potatoes.

New Potatoes with Spinach in Lemon and Yogurt Dressing

1½ **pounds new potatoes**
12 **spinach leaves, shredded**
½ **bunch spring onions, chopped**
juice of ½ **lemon**
5 **ounces natural yogurt**
salt and black pepper to taste

Potatoes and spinach make splendid bedfellows. The stringent, slightly bitter taste of the spinach gives the rather dour-tasting potatoes a necessary lift.

The spinach will have remained dormant all winter, but as soon as the weather begins to improve the new leaves shoot up. If you have bought spinach for another meal, select the smaller, fresher leaves for this salad. Use slightly larger new potatoes rather than the very small ones.

Cook the potatoes as described in the recipe above and allow them to cool. Set aside a small amount of shredded spinach leaves and spring onions for garnishing, and then combine the remaining ingredients with the potatoes in a serving bowl. Mix well, garnish with reserved spinach and spring onions, and serve.

1–2 pounds asparagus (amount depends on your purse)
4 eggs (fertile if possible)
sea salt to taste

Asparagus is one of the delights of the year, and although it may be expensive you don't have to have filet mignon to accompany it. Nor does it have to be just a starter to a multi-course meal. For a feast that won't cost you a fortune, accompany this recipe with Minted New Potatoes (page 37) or some good wholegrain bread, and a plain green salad of crisp chilled Romaine lettuce leaves.

Prepare the asparagus as described on page 11 and put it on to cook. It will take an average of 10 minutes, but a lot will depend on your cooking method and on the thickness of the stalks. To be sure of not overcooking it, stand guard over the pan.

Five to six minutes before you think the asparagus will be cooked (eggs mollet are halfway between soft-boiled and hard-boiled), gently lower the eggs into medium boiling water. Now gather your friends or family around your dining table and serve the asparagus on one large warm plate as soon as it is cooked. Place the eggs in egg cups alongside the spears. Don't bother to peel the eggs, but just cut off the tops. Each person simply dips their asparagus into the eggs and then seasons it with salt, as required.

Dill, Pea, and Potato Salad

1 pound small potatoes, cooked
8 ounces fresh garden peas,
    lightly cooked
2 tablespoons chopped fresh
    dill weed
3 tablespoons vegetable oil
1 tablespoon lemon juice or
    white wine vinegar
1 teaspoon French mustard
2 fluid ounces cream (optional)
salt and pepper to taste
3 or 4 dill flower heads to
    garnish (optional)

Fresh dill goes well with potatoes, eggs, pickled fish, cream, and of course, pickled gherkins or cucumbers. These can be combined on a bed of lettuce hearts to make a grand salad in the Nicoise style, but far more frequently we would use it in this simple salad.

Cut the potatoes into bite-sized pieces, turn them into a mixing bowl, and add the garden peas. Beat or blend together the dill, oil, lemon juice, mustard, and the cream, if used. Season the dressing with salt and pepper and pour it over the potatoes and peas.

Mix together all the ingredients, turn them into a serving bowl, and garnish with the dill flowers.

Chicory with Croûtons and Sesame Seeds

SERVES 4 to 6

1 head of chicory (or escarole),
    trimmed of all coarse outer
    leaves and well washed
4 tablespoons Vinaigrette
    Dressing, preferably made
    with walnut or olive oil
2 tablespoons whipping cream
1 large clove garlic, well crushed
1 tablespoon freshly toasted
    sesame seeds
36 traditional croûtons (page 131)

We like the sheer untidiness of chicory. A few leaves curling and twisting in all directions can fill a salad bowl. Its robust bitter flavor is best accompanied by other strong flavors.

Break the chicory leaves off the head and place them in a large salad bowl. Taste the darker green leaves and discard them if they are too bitter.

Beat the vinaigrette, the cream, and the crushed garlic together into a smooth emulsion. Pour two-thirds of this dressing over the chicory and toss thoroughly until all the leaves are well coated. Sprinkle the toasted sesame seeds evenly over the dressed leaves. Add the croûtons to the remaining dressing, toss them well, and then scatter them over the salad.

Our Coleslaw

½ small white drumhead
   (16-ounce) or Savoy cabbage,
   stripped of all loose, dirty, or
   damaged leaves
2–3 medium carrots, peeled,
   grated, or cut into rounds
½ small onion, very finely
   chopped
salt and black pepper
10–12 caraway seeds
5 fluid ounces Mayonnaise
   (page 126)

True coleslaw is not that commonly seen travesty, rough-chopped cabbage, colored with grated carrot and sunk in a vinegary mayonnaise-type dressing. When making coleslaw, strive to protect the unique character of the drumhead cabbage. No other vegetable has quite that crunch, or a heart of such tightly clasped leaves that can be cut into such attractive, slender, corrugated sections. Try these finely cut leaves tossed with just a handful of freshly grated carrot and a touch of chopped onion, seasoned with salt, pepper, and a few caraway seeds. We prefer it without a liquid dressing at all, but by all means, add mayonnaise if you wish. Do not, however, use a plain vinaigrette dressing or the cabbage will very quickly become translucent and unattractive to look at.

A visually attractive salad can be made from the hearts of Savoy cabbage. The leaves are even more corrugated than those of the drumhead and the soft green color goes beautifully with the orange of the carrot. Emphasize this by cutting the carrot into paper-thin rounds. This is most simply done on the fine slicing attachment of a food processor, or otherwise with a very sharp knife.

Cut away any coarse protruding ribs from the cabbage, cut it into quarters and remove the stem sections. Very finely slice the cabbage quarters into long shreds, either by hand or in a machine. Discard any unattractive-looking sections. Thoroughly combine all the ingredients in a mixing bowl. Adjust the seasoning.

**5 ounces Cilantro Cream Sauce
(page 135)
4 hard-boiled eggs, quartered
4 ounces white button
mushrooms, stalks trimmed off
juice of ½ lemon
about 20 black olives
4 sprigs of cilantro to garnish**

We've given two versions of this recipe. The first is colorful and elegant and makes egg mayonnaise look like a country bumpkin! The second version makes a cheerful, wholesome, filling bowl salad.

Take 4 plain white side plates. Place a good heaped tablespoon of the green cilantro sauce in the center of each. Arrange the quartered eggs, yellow side up, around this.

Finely slice the mushrooms and place them around the eggs. Dress the mushroom slices with lemon juice. Scatter the black olives over the plates and garnish the completed salad with the cilantro sprigs.

VARIATION

**12 fluid ounces Cilantro Cream
Sauce (page 135)
12 ounces cooked macaroni or
pasta shells
4 ounces white button
mushrooms, quartered
juice of 1 small lemon
about 20 black olives
4 hard-boiled eggs, quartered
roughly chopped cilantro
leaves to garnish**

Place the sauce, macaroni, mushrooms, and lemon juice in a bowl and mix well. Gently fold in the eggs and the olives. Turn into a serving bowl and garnish with the chopped cilantro leaves.

Strawberry and Cucumber Salad

half a cucumber (about 8 ounces)
salt and black pepper to taste
6 ounces strawberries, washed,
    drained, and hulled
juice of ½ lime

This cheerful, light, formal salad brings with it the promise of better days to come. The first strawberries always make a special impact and when used like this, a few go far. Often those first fruits are quite tart and are better treated this way than served as a dessert. Lime juice has just the correct balance of sweetness and acidity to enhance both the main ingredients.

A fine side salad to accompany poached mackerel or cold cooked poultry.

Peel the cucumber and slice it wafer-thin. Spread these slices in concentric circles over 4 individual plates. Lightly dust the cucumber with salt and black pepper. Quarter the strawberries and pile them in the center of each plate. Dress with the lime juice and chill before serving.

Minted Belgian Endive Salad

½ small head lettuce, shredded
½ medium Spanish onion, finely
    sliced
2 heads prepared Belgian endive,
    cut into ¾-inch slices
1 sweet orange, peeled, sliced,
    and chopped
2 tablespoons fresh mint,
    chopped
2 tablespoons Vinaigrette
    Dressing (page 125)

Belgian endive is a very useful salad vegetable so long as its slight bitterness is carefully complemented by the other ingredients. In this salad we cover a gamut of flavors ranging from the bitterness of the Belgian endive to the sweetness of the orange.

Layer the lettuce in the bottom of a salad bowl. Combine the other ingredients in a mixing bowl and toss them well together. Mound this salad on top of the lettuce leaves and serve.

Belgian Endive, Avocado, and Watercress Salad in Orange Vinaigrette

1 small avocado, peeled and
   chopped
½ bunch watercress, shredded
3 heads of prepared Belgian
   endive, cut into ¾-inch slices
2 tablespoons Vinaigrette
   Dressing (page 125)
salt and black pepper to taste
2 tablespoons fresh orange juice
orange slices to garnish

The mildly bitter taste of the Belgian endive contrasts well with the slight sweetness of both the avocado and the orange dressing, and the greens of the salad and the bright garnish are very appetizing.

Combine the avocado, watercress and Belgian endive in a salad bowl. Mix together the vinaigrette and orange juice and pour it over the salad. Season to taste. Toss the salad gently and serve garnished with four orange slices.

Baby Turnips in Horseradish Cream Sauce

1 bunch (about 1 pound) fresh
   young white turnips
2 tablespoons horseradish sauce
2 tablespoons whipping cream
lemon juice to taste
salt and black pepper to taste

Turnips are often the first of the locally grown outdoor crops to be ready for eating. Use only small firm turnips for salads. Reject any roots that are soft and spongy. This is a simple salad but a first rate one to accompany cold pork or beef, or it could be served as one of a selection of salads.

Peel and grate the turnips. If they are soggy, toss them in a clean cloth and squeeze out excess moisture. Put the turnips into a serving bowl and stir in other ingredients. Test for seasoning and serve.

Artichokes are such a tasty seasonal treat that, provided they are fresh, they are not to be missed. For a dinner party, they make a trouble-free appetizer, the eating of which is bound to unfreeze the most formal gathering since it is quite impossible to eat them in an over-dignified manner. They also give the quieter of your guests a chance to say something while the more loquacious have their mouths occupied. Place a large bowl or plate in the center of the table for everyone to throw in their discarded leaves and any inedible chokes. This way every guest ends up with a clean plate and doesn't have to make excuses to the host or hostess if artichokes are not their favorite food. Remember, it is the interesting flavor you are serving; there is often very little flesh on artichokes. People certainly don't get fat on them, so follow up with a substantial main course.

Allow 2 small or 1 large artichoke per person and prepare and cook them as described on page 10. Stand the cooked artichokes upside down to drain and cool.

Serve lukewarm with a choice of dressings, for example: a lemon-flavored mayonnaise and a vinaigrette dressing made with olive oil and thick cream, seasoned with salt and pepper and sharpened with lemon juice.

Snow Pea and Avocado Salad

SERVES 4 TO 6

1 pound snow peas (top and tail
    and remove strings, if
    necessary)
2 small to medium avocados,
    peeled and chopped small
2 ounces small fresh mushrooms,
    finely sliced
2 tablespoons olive oil
1 tablespoon lemon juice
salt and black pepper
2 tablespoons parsley, finely
    chopped, to garnish

*If the snow peas are very young and tender, just top and tail
them and use them raw in the salad. If a little older, boil them
very briefly as directed in the recipe. Snow peas deteriorate very
quickly, so buy only the freshest, flat pods (any pods in which the
peas have been allowed to develop will already be stringy and
starchy). Finally, if in doubt, don't buy them; they're expensive.*

Either use raw snow peas or drop them into a pan of boiling
water and boil for 2–3 minutes, drain them, and rinse under cold water.
    Combine the peas, avocados, mushrooms, olive oil, lemon juice,
salt, and black pepper, and toss them well together. Garnish with
parsley and serve.

Broccoli with Lemon Egg Mayonnaise

1 pound broccoli separated into
    florets, stalks cut to about
    4 inches in length
1 tablespoon lemon juice
2 hard-boiled eggs, finely chopped
4 fluid ounces Mayonnaise
    (page 126)

Place the broccoli in a pan of rapidly boiling salted water
sufficient just to cover. Cook for 6–8 minutes. Drain, cool under
cold running water, and drain again. Whisk the lemon juice and
chopped egg into the mayonnaise and pour over the broccoli. Serve.

1½ **pounds prepared leeks**
salt to taste
3 fluid ounces Mayonnaise
  (page 126)
3 fluid ounces sour cream
2 or 3 spring onions, finely
  chopped
2 tablespoons finely chopped
  parsley
black pepper

For this recipe the little finger-thick leeks available in late spring-time are a delight. Unfortunately, this "poor man's asparagus" is difficult to obtain. There is no real reason for this, as we grow plenty of leeks on to full size. If you live in the country, you may have more success than town folk in finding the young vegetables. When they are obtainable, they are very reasonably priced and well worth pursuing.

Place the leeks horizontally in a pan of rapidly boiling salted water sufficient just to cover them. Cook for 6–8 minutes or until a table fork can pierce the white flesh. Cool immediately under cold running water. Drain.

Combine the mayonnaise, sour cream, and spring onions. Arrange the leeks in a shallow serving dish and pour over the dressing. Garnish with parsley and serve.

VARIATION

For a thinner sauce and slightly sharper taste, replace the mayonnaise with the same amount of Vinaigrette Dressing (page 125).

Avocado and Red Cabbage Salad

18 ounces red cabbage, outer
    leaves and coarse ribs removed
2 ripe but firm avocados
2 tablespoons plus 1 teaspoon
    sesame seeds, freshly toasted
salt and black pepper to taste
Vinaigrette Dressing (page 125)

A friend and regular customer who had spent some time in Israel returned raving about this salad, which she said she had eaten almost every day of her stay there. To us, it seemed an unlikely combination, but after being induced to try it, we were converted. The secret lies in the toasted sesame seeds, which transform this salad.

Finely slice or shred the red cabbage and place it in a large mixing bowl. Halve the avocados, remove the pits, peel, and then dice the flesh before adding it to the cabbage. Add 2 tablespoons toasted sesame seeds, the salt, pepper, and the vinaigrette, and toss well together. Turn into a serving bowl and sprinkle with the remaining sesame seeds.

Avocado and Pink Grapefruit Salad

4 medium Haas avocados, peeled
    and sliced
salt and freshly ground black
    pepper
2 pink grapefruit, peeled, with
    all traces of pith removed
4 tablespoons oil
4 teaspoons wine or cider vinegar

A salad of simple contrasts, soft green set against soft pink. The almost excessive richness of the avocado is cut here by the tartness of the grapefruit, which in its turn is made to taste sweet by having dribbled over it at the last moment a small quantity of even sharper vinegar.

Arrange the slices of avocado radial fashion on 4 small plain plates. Season well with the salt and black pepper.

Separate the grapefruit into segments and cut each segment in half. Pile these half segments in the center of each plate. Dress the salad with oil and, just before serving, sprinkle the grapefruit with the vinegar.

Spinach and Walnut Salad with Mint and Lemon Dressing

4 ounces young spinach leaves—
  discard any damaged or
  discolored leaves
2–3 spring onions, chopped
2 tablespoons chopped walnuts,
  lightly toasted
2 tablespoons olive oil
1 tablespoon lemon juice
1 tablespoon fresh mint, finely
  chopped
salt and black pepper to taste

Tender young spinach leaves available in the late spring can be used to make a green salad. The pale green leaves (the paler the better—bitterness increases as the leaves darken) have a surprisingly mild flavor and are, of course, most nutritious. The toasted walnuts in the recipe give the salad an unexpected crunch.

Wash the spinach leaves individually and carefully cut off the stems, and chop the leaves into very thin shreds. Mix them with the spring onions and walnuts. Combine the olive oil, lemon juice, mint, salt, and black pepper to taste and mix well. Toss the salad in this dressing and serve.

Avocado and Yogurt Salad

2 medium-sized avocados
8 fluid ounces natural yogurt
1 clove garlic, finely chopped
1 tablespoon walnuts, chopped
salt to taste
sprigs of parsley for garnish
black pepper

Prepare this salad with firm but not underripe avocados. Smooth-skinned avocados should give just a little if gently squeezed between finger and thumb, but they will be quite soft around the neck. The alligator-skinned Haas avocados can be softer, but don't buy them if the skin has begun to shrink.

Peel the avocados and cut the flesh into medium-sized chunks. Put the yogurt in a serving bowl and stir in the garlic, walnuts, and salt to taste. Stir in the avocado chunks, garnish with sprigs of parsley, and finish off the salad with a few grindings of black pepper.

Chicory and Walnut Salad

1 pound chicory leaves
2 ounces walnuts, chopped
2 teaspoons French mustard
2 tablespoons olive oil
1 tablespoon wine vinegar
salt and black pepper to taste

The curly mop-headed chicory available in winter and spring has a faintly bitter flavor that sharpens the taste buds. Try this salad as a starter or side salad.

Discard any damaged or discolored chicory leaves, trim the stems off, wash the leaves one by one, and drain them. Put the leaves in a salad bowl with the nuts. Put the mustard in a small bowl and slowly beat in the oil. Stir in the vinegar and salt and pepper to taste. Pour the dressing over the salad, toss well, and serve.

Celeriac Rémoulade

1 large celeriac root (1 pound)
lemon juice or vinegar
5 ounce Mayonnaise (page 126)
1 tablespoon French mustard
2 teaspoons white wine vinegar
    or lemon juice
salt and pepper to taste
1 fluid ounce thick cream
    (optional)

Plain looking but very tasty, celeriac rémoulade is one of the most popular constituents of the traditional vegetable crudités *presented in countless small eating places in France. The recipe does not demand great exactness, the celeriac, mustard, mayonnaise, and vinegar being happy companions. Soften the taste with cream if you like.*

Peel the celeriac root, cutting away any brown patches. Finely slice or shred the root into long matchsticks. Put these directly into a bowl of cold water acidulated with lemon juice or vinegar. When all the celeriac is prepared, blanch it by dropping it into a pan of boiling water for no more than a minute. Drain well and mix with the rest of the ingredients. Set the salad aside in a cool place to let the flavors intermingle for at least two hours.

Asparagus with Sesame Seed and Soy Dressing

20 spears of asparagus, trimmed,
   cut into 1½-inch lengths
salt
4 tablespoons Sesame Seed and
   Soy Dressing (page 141)

In this Japanese-inspired recipe, the asparagus is only parcooked. If you prefer softer-cooked asparagus (although it should always retain some "bite"), increase the cooking time given by 3 to 4 minutes.

Drop the asparagus into a pan of slow boiling salted water, cook for 5 minutes, and drain. Rinse immediately under cold water until the asparagus is cooled. Drain. Put the dressing in a mixing bowl, add the asparagus, and toss together lightly. Divide the asparagus lengths between four small bowls and serve.

Spiced Potato Salad with Fresh Cilantro Leaves

A hot, spicy salad that keeps well and tastes even better the day after preparation.

1½ pounds potatoes, peeled and
   grated, or use small, new whole
   potatoes, washed
2 tablespoons sesame seed oil or
   other vegetable oil
2 ounces sesame seeds
1 tablespoon mustard seeds
1 inch fresh ginger root, peeled
   and finely grated
½ teaspoon chili powder or
   hot pepper sauce
salt to taste
juice of ½ lemon
2 tablespoons fresh cilantro
   leaves, chopped

Put the potatoes in a pan with plenty of boiling water and boil them until only just tender. Remove from the heat, drain, and put into a salad bowl.

Heat the oil in a frying pan and stir in the sesame seeds, ginger, chili powder, and salt to taste. Stir-fry over moderate heat for 3–4 minutes. Stir the oil and spices into the potatoes, add the lemon juice, and mix well. Allow to cool completely.

Gently stir in the cilantro leaves. Serve or chill for later use.

Kaleidoscope Salad

**9 ounces bean sprouts, rinsed
and drained**
**1 bunch watercress, washed and
drained**
2 slices pineapple
**1 small sweet red pepper, halved
and seeded**
**1 tablespoon tamari (natural soy
sauce)**

*A colorful alternative to green salad with good clean colors
and simple flavor contrasts. Once you have the ingredients it is
very quick to assemble. Preselected and washed watercress and bean
sprouts are available in sealed packages from many supermarkets.
We would prefer to use fresh pineapple, but the canned fruit is a fair
substitute.*

Place the bean sprouts in a mixing bowl. Remove any roots and
coarse stems from the watercress. Lightly chop the remaining stems and
leaves and add these to the bean sprouts. Cut the pineapple up into
small chunks over the bean sprouts and watercress so that they catch
any juice that runs free. Slice the red pepper into thin strips and add
these to the rest of the ingredients.

Spoon the tamari over all. Toss this salad very thoroughly so that
all the ingredients become well coated.

Watercress and Radish Salad

**1 bunch watercress—discard
yellow leaves, trim the stems,
wash, and drain**
**1 bunch radishes, trimmed,
washed, drained, and chilled
for 1 hour or more**
**½ small head of lettuce, washed
and drained (use hearts of
iceberg lettuce or small
Romaine lettuce)**
Vinaigrette Dressing (page 125)

*A delicate-looking but strongly flavored salad. Use the freshest
watercress and the crunchiest radishes you can find.*

Make a bed of lettuce leaves in rosette fashion in a serving bowl
and sprinkle over a little dressing. Thinly slice the radishes and combine
them with the watercress. Add Vinaigrette Dressing to taste and toss
the mixture in it. Arrange the dressed radish and watercress on the
lettuce leaves and serve.

2 ounces Blue Stilton or other blue cheese
4 fluid ounces whipping cream
4 teaspoons wine or cider vinegar
salt to taste
tight hearts of 1 large or 2 small iceberg lettuces
1 tablespoon chopped chives for garnish
16 walnut halves for garnish

There are other ways of serving lettuce than in a tossed green salad. Try one of these recipes.

CREAMY BLUE CHEESE DRESSING

Crumble the cheese into a small mixing bowl, and add the cream and the vinegar. Gently whisk these together until all but a few crumbs of cheese have disappeared. Salt to taste if necessary. Set aside.

Neatly quarter the lettuce hearts so that the leaves remain attached to the core. Wash them, peeling back the leaves to check that no dirt or insects remain trapped. Shake the lettuce hearts dry and divide them, cut side up, on four side plates. Pour the dressing over all and garnish with the chives and walnuts. Serve immediately.

3½ fluid ounces mayonnaise
3½ fluid ounces natural yogurt
salt and pepper
½ medium onion, cut into rings
2 hard-boiled eggs, peeled and sliced
8 green olives
1 tablespoon chopped chervil for garnish (optional)

EGG AND OLIVE DRESSING

Whisk the mayonnaise and yogurt together. Season if necessary. Carefully fold in the onion rings and the sliced eggs. Divide this sauce between the lettuce hearts and garnish them with the olives and chervil. Serve immediately.

1 pound white cabbage, finely
  shredded
1 bunch radishes, topped, tailed,
  and thinly sliced
salt
3 tablespoons sesame seed oil or
  other vegetable oil
½ fresh or dried chili pepper,
  seeds removed, finely chopped
2 teaspoons freshly ground
  coriander seeds
1 tablespoon coarsely chopped
  cilantro leaves (optional)

A Chinese-inspired cold salad with flavorings like chili and sesame.

Combine the cabbage and radishes and salt to taste. Heat the oil in a small pan and stir in the chili and coriander. Cook and stir for 2 minutes and then stir the spiced oil into the cabbage and radish mixture. Sprinkle with cilantro leaves, if available, and serve.

VARIATION

In Chinese cookery, the cabbage and radish mixture would be liberally sprinkled with salt and set aside for 3–5 hours. The mixture is then rinsed and pressed before being mixed with spiced oil.

Summer Salads

During the summer, everything is in the salad maker's favor—every week brings a new vegetable into season, and every trip to the market means a new discovery. Although we may lose one or two short-season vegetables, as time passes there is a steady accumulation of produce. From midsummer on, there is little need to buy anything that isn't locally grown; but that doesn't mean northern gardeners have to isolate themselves totally from the produce of warmer regions. Summer days bring, for example, the apple-like sweetness of Vidalia onions from Georgia, the richness of California avocados, and, of course, vegetables and fruits like eggplants, melons, and peaches, that are earlier and tastier when grown in warmer climates.

With such a choice it pays to buy with discretion. Shop around, choose the freshest produce, and don't buy too much, since vegetables spoil quickly in warm weather. Be careful about buying too many bargains during the summer. They have to be used immediately and you don't save much when everything else is relatively cheap. Leaf vegetables past their prime are never a bargain, and sorting through faded fruit and vegetables is always a thankless, time-consuming task. Chide your produce manager if something is not up to scratch. Compliment them when it's particularly pleasing. Such information is useful to them when they next go to market. At this time of the year they, too, can shop around. For quality and economy, here is a broad outline of what to look out for as the season progresses.

Early summer. Southern zucchini, garden lettuce, broad beans, carrots, beets, and garden peas.

Midsummer. Zucchini, fresh garlic, green beans, plum tomatoes, Spanish onions, new potatoes, tomatoes.

Late summer. Pole and runner beans, broccoli, Italian fennel, peppers, corn on the cob, apples, melons, celery, cauliflower.

Summer herbs. A few pots growing herbs can transform the range and flavors of summer salads. Keep basil in a sunny window spot, parsley, mint, chives, and tarragon in well-watered pots outside. Given just a tiny plot of land, dill, chervil, and fennel will more than earn their keep. That same little plot can also be used to grow the rediscovered salad herbs, such as cress, sorrel, lamb's lettuce, and hyssop, which can give interest and distinction to green salads, not just in summer, but all the year round.

Green salads should change like the seasons. Summer green salads can be bright and colorful and good-looking enough to act as table decoration. For instance, pile a multitude of torn leaves into a big white or glass bowl and scatter the flowers of herb plants across the top. People who grow some of their own salad ingredients are often looking for ways of using them up. Try decorating your table with them, not your compost heap. Even if you have to buy all your salad goods, they are cheap enough in middle and late summer for you to be carefree in their use.

Here are some thoughts on summer greens and a suggestion for a green leaf salad.

Romaine and iceberg lettuce. *Long leaves and round leaves, cool and crisp.*

Watercress. *Spicy, peppery, dark green leaf.*

Sorrel. *Astringent, tangy almost lemony flavor; home-grown or picked on a walk in the park or country.*

Basil. *Peppery strings of tiny leaves from bush basil; grow in a sunny spot.*

Cress. *Pungent, finely cut leaves. Easily homegrown.*

Hyssop. *A piquant bitterness, not to be overdone; easily grown in pot or garden.*

Carefully wash summer green leaves under cold running water. Gently tear up the larger leaves. Dress and toss them just before serving with a vinaigrette of olive or walnut oil made with a low proportion of vinegar or lemon juice (4–5 parts oil to 1 part lemon).

Garnish the salad with the mild-flavored flowers of hyssop, peppery golden nasturtium flowers, and the beautiful blue borage.

Poor Boy Salad

SERVES 8

14 ounces tomatoes, juice and
    seeds removed, diced
½ medium cucumber, diced
1 large pickled gherkin, diced
1 sweet red pepper, cored and
    seeded, diced
1 medium onion, diced, or 4 large
    spring onions, including half
    the green part, sliced
One or two of the following par-
    boiled vegetables (4 ounces of
    each): cauliflower, broccoli,
    young green beans, asparagus
    tips, or artichoke hearts,
    chopped
2 tablespoons capers
4 ounces green olives, pitted
½ bunch parsley, chopped
2 large cloves garlic, crushed
4 fluid ounces olive oil
2 tablespoons wine vinegar
2 teaspoons French mustard
2 teaspoons dried oregano
salt and black pepper to taste

This salad can be found in Italian, Creole, and black restaurants in New Orleans, in South America, and in the Caribbean. Serve it with grilled or roasted meats. It is wonderful with barbecued food. This salad should be made the day before it is to be eaten and will store well for days.

In New Orleans, sandwiches are called poor boys— "Poor boy, he can only afford sandwiches." A popular Italian version is the submarine, 10 inches round by 3 inches high, stuffed with salad, salami, cheese with ham—some poor boy!

Place all the ingredients in a mixing bowl. Stir well, adjust the seasoning, cover, and leave to mature in a cool place for 24 hours.

Cucumber with Sesame Ginger Dressing

2 tablespoons tahini
2 tablespoons natural yogurt or
    water
1 tablespoon sesame oil
1 teaspoon vinegar
1 teaspoon tamari or soy sauce
1 clove garlic, crushed
1 almond-sized piece of fresh
    ginger, peeled and crushed
dash of hot pepper sauce
black pepper to taste
½ large cucumber
1 teaspoon sesame seeds to
    garnish

This nutty dip is good with any vegetable crudités, *but it is especially good with cucumber. The sweet sesame oil is an important constituent of this dressing so it is best not to substitute for it.*

Combine all the ingredients except the cucumber and sesame seeds in a small bowl. Mix together well and pile the mixture in the center of a large serving plate.

Cut the cucumber down the middle and remove the seeds with the back of a teaspoon. Cut the cucumber into strips 3 inches long and arrange these in and around the mound of dressing like the spokes of a wheel. Sprinkle with sesame seeds.

VARIATION

Use 12 ounces bean sprouts instead of cucumber. Stir the shoots well into the dressing and then sprinkle with the sesame seeds.

Cucumber and Thick Yogurt Dressing

salt
½ cucumber, deseeded and
    finely chopped
10 fluid ounces Strained Natural
    Yogurt (page 128)
1 clove garlic, crushed
8 fresh mint leaves, finely
    chopped
½ teaspoon dry-roasted and
    ground cumin seed (optional)
sprigs of mint to garnish

Cucumber and yogurt are a winning combination. Flavored with garlic, mint, and cumin they appear throughout the Middle East in many forms under such names as raita, cacik, tzatziki, *or* jajig. *This deluxe version is closest to the Greek* tzatziki. *If you haven't the time to drain the yogurt or deseed the cucumber don't worry; it will still taste good, but it is then best eaten as soon as prepared.*

Scatter the salt over the cucumber and place it in a colander to drain for 30 minutes. Lightly press out any excess moisture and place the cucumber in a mixing bowl. Stir in the remaining ingredients, check for seasoning and transfer to a serving dish. Garnish with sprigs of mint.

Simple Carrot Salad

1 pound young carrots, scrubbed
   and finely grated
2 tablespoons olive oil
1 tablespoon lemon juice
salt to taste

This most simple of salads is at its best made with the sweet baby carrots available in late June and early July.

Combine all the ingredients. Toss well and serve.

VARIATION

Add a handful of chopped fresh parsley, fresh fennel, or fresh chervil.

Nouvelle Cuisine Crudités

Meals are often memorable not just for the food that was served but also for the manner in which it was presented. One such occasion Paddy cherishes took place one lunchtime outside a small restaurant in a picturesque hill village in southern France.

The diners were a group of models and their photographers (it was that picturesque a village). The party of eight were gathered round a large, rough, wooden table. On went the white paper table-cloths and everyone was given a fork and a small cutting board. In quick succession the table was spread with bowls of different dressings, a jug of thick cream, seasonings, crusty country loaves, glasses, pitchers of chilled white wine, a large vine rootstock hung with small salami sausages and sharp knives dangling from small leather thongs, a plate of tiny green beans and, finally, as center piece and main edible attraction, a great flower basket decoratively arranged with gleaming whole vegetables: red peppers, green peppers, tiny cauliflowers and cucumbers, quartered fennel bulbs, celery hearts, tomatoes, bouquets of fresh herbs, and a pile of lemons. The diners were then left to compose and dress their salads to their own liking. It kept them busy—but not quiet—for an hour.

Romaine Salad in Fennel Cream Dressing

2 teaspoons finely chopped fresh
   fennel leaves
8 fluid ounces light cream
2 teaspoons lemon juice
salt and black pepper to taste
1 medium-sized Romaine lettuce,
   washed, dried well, and
   coarsely chopped

A simple variation on green salad in vinaigrette dressing using fresh fennel leaves. These are the delicate, feathery leaves from common fennel, one of the most imposing plants to be found in an herb garden. You can, of course, use other fresh herbs or mixed herbs in this dressing.

Combine all ingredients. Toss well and serve.

Caribbean Summer Salad

4-inch piece of cucumber,
   quartered lengthwise and
   chopped crosswise
2 medium-sized just-ripe bananas,
   thinly sliced
2 medium-sized green peppers,
   seeded, cored, and diced
2 sweet oranges, peeled, pith
   removed, separated into
   segments and cut into halves
5 fluid ounces natural yogurt
1 tablespoon flaked almonds,
   lightly toasted

A salad that can be made all the year round but is cooling and refreshingly sweet on a very hot summer's day. It is also good as an exotic and colorful starter for a winter meal that needs cheering up.

Combine the cucumber, banana, green pepper, and oranges in a salad bowl. Stir in the yogurt, sprinkle almonds over the top, chill, and serve.

Guacamole

SERVES 4 TO 6

2 large ripe avocados (the flesh
    soft but not discolored)
1 beefsteak tomato or 2 large
    ordinary tomatoes, peeled,
    seeded, juiced, and chopped
2 tablespoons chopped onion
    (white of spring onions is best)
1 tablespoon chopped fresh
    green cilantro leaves
1 tablespoon lemon or lime juice
1 clove garlic, chopped very fine
1 fresh chili pepper, seeded and
    chopped very fine, or hot
    pepper sauce to taste
1 teaspoon paprika (optional)
salt and pepper to taste
5 fluid ounces sour cream or
    yogurt

Paddy was just beginning to relax after completing a small, pleasant country wedding lunch when one of the guests approached and said, "Doo tell me what that wonderful green slime was...so-oh delicious." Well, it was guacamole—this Mexican, spiced, creamy avocado sauce that can be used as a dip for raw or parboiled vegetables, as an accompaniment to fish and chicken, or as an appetizer with sour cream and corn tortilla chips or fresh bread.

Guacamole quickly deteriorates once it has been made, for avocado blackens in the air. If you have any left over, you can extend its life by almost filling a small container with it, adding a stone from the avocado, and then sealing the top with a thin layer of oil. When you want to serve the guacamole, pour off the excess oil, discard the stone, and stir in any oil that remains on the surface.

Peel and dice the avocados and turn them into a steep-sided mixing bowl. Add all the other ingredients except the sour cream, and mix well (but not so well that every trace of the separate ingredients disappears).

Spoon the salad onto individual plates. Top with a spoonful of the sour cream, decoratively stirred in with a single spiral turn of the spoon.

Simple Green Bean Salad in Lemon Dressing

1 pound young green beans,
    topped only
salt
4 tablespoons olive oil
2 tablespoons lemon juice
black pepper
2 ounces black olives (pit and
    chop 4 or 5 olives and leave
    the rest whole)

Young green beans at their best should be crisp and snap easily when broken in two. They need only a minimum of cooking and the cooked beans should still have some crunch.

Put the beans in a large pan of salted boiling water and cook for 10 minutes or less. Drain them, rinse immediately under cold running water, drain again, and then put them into a salad bowl. Add the oil, lemon juice, black pepper, and whole olives. Toss well and chill slightly before serving garnished with the chopped olives.

VARIATION

For a more substantial salad, add 2 or 3 quartered hard-boiled eggs to the salad before serving.

Green Beans and Sweet Corn with Tomato Mayonnaise

8 ounces green beans
3-ounce can sweet corn kernels
    (or 1 large ear of corn, cooked
    and scraped)
2 ripe tomatoes
5 fluid ounces Mayonnaise
    (page 126)
salt and black pepper to taste

A pretty, mild-flavored salad as welcome in late spring, made from southern beans and canned sweet corn, as it is in late summer, made with fresh homegrown vegetables.

Top and tail the beans and drop them into a saucepan of rapidly boiling salted water for 4–6 minutes, until cooked but still retaining a little bite. Drain and cool immediately under running water. Cut the cooked green beans into 2-inch lengths and set them aside.

Cut the tomatoes in half and shake out the seeds and the excess juice. Chop the flesh up finely and put it into a small mixing bowl. Pour in the mayonnaise and with a fork beat together until the mayonnaise is well colored. Add the green beans and corn, seasoned with salt and pepper, mix well, and serve.

Okra with Horseradish and Soy Sauce Dressing

20 pods young okra, washed well,
  stalk ends trimmed off (do not
  expose the seeds)
2 tablespoons prepared horseradish sauce
3 tablespoons tamari (natural
  soy sauce)

We find okra difficult to use as a salad vegetable because the mature pod gets too sticky and fibrous, so this dish is only worthwhile if you have very young, tender okra. It goes particularly well with plain grilled or fried fish.

Cook the okra in a pan of gently boiling, lightly salted water for 3–4 minutes only. Drain and immediately rinse under cold running water until cooled.

Cut the okra diagonally into ½-inch lengths. Divide the pieces between 4 shallow serving dishes, making a mound in the center of each dish. Mix together the horseradish and soy sauce and sprinkle the dressing over the okra.

VARIATION

Cook the okra as indicated above and serve with Basic Tomato Sauce (page 129).

Zucchini and Parsley Salad

1½ pounds small zucchini
2 tablespoons sunflower oil or
  butter
4 tablespoons Vinaigrette
  Dressing (page 125)
3 tablespoons fresh parsley,
  coarsely chopped
1 teaspoon dill seeds (optional)
salt and pepper to taste

A very simple but effective zucchini salad. The recipe calls for dill seeds but you could use the dill seed heads retrieved from a jar of dill pickles.

Cook the zucchini in the oil or butter, as in the recipe above, then chill them completely under cold running water. Pat dry, then place them in a serving bowl. Add the remaining ingredients, toss them well together, and serve.

Zucchini, Dill, and Yogurt Salad

2 tablespoons sunflower oil or
  butter
1½ pounds small zucchini,
  topped and tailed, cut into
  ½-inch rounds
2 teaspoons fresh dill, chopped
4 fluid ounces natural yogurt
1 tablespoon lemon juice
salt and black pepper to taste
pinch paprika

Both the leaves and the seeds of the dill plant, a member of the parsley family, are used in cooking. The dried seeds have a more pungent flavor than the leaves, which can be used fresh or dried. In this recipe we use fresh dill leaves (also called dill weed), because their milder flavor suits the yogurt sauce better. For a special garnish, use whole dill flowers or the immature seed heads. They are most attractive.

Heat the oil or butter in a pan and add the zucchini. Stir in the dill (reserving small pinch for garnish later) and cover the pan. Cook over a moderate heat, stirring occasionally for 5–8 minutes until the zucchini are barely tender, but firm to the bite.

Transfer the contents of the pan to a bowl and allow the zucchini to cool a little. Stir in the yogurt, lemon juice, salt, and black pepper. Turn the zucchini and sauce into a serving bowl and garnish with a pinch of paprika and the reserved dill. Serve.

VARIATION

This salad can be made with dried dill when fresh is unavailable.

Zucchini in Olive Oil and Lemon Dressing

2–3 tablespoons olive oil
juice of ½ lemon
½ teaspoon brown sugar
salt and black pepper to taste
1–1½ pound small zucchini

This side salad is best served with the dressing poured on it at the last moment. Broccoli can be prepared in the same manner.

The aromatic oil gives off an evocative scent of summer climes as it is poured over the warm vegetables.

Combine the olive oil, lemon juice, sugar, and seasoning to taste. Mix well and set aside.

Cook the zucchini whole in a pan of rapidly boiling water for 8–10 minutes. Test one for readiness by giving a gentle squeeze—if it gives a little, it is cooked. Drain and cool the zucchini briefly under running cold water. (This enables you to handle them more easily, and it also helps keep the skins bright green.)

Top and tail the zucchini and cut them up into ½-inch rounds. Place them in a serving bowl. Pour over the dressing, mix well, check the seasoning, and serve immediately.

Hot Potato Salad

1½ pounds new potatoes
2 tablespoons finely chopped onion
3 tablespoons olive oil
1 tablespoon wine vinegar
salt and black pepper to taste
4 tablespoons chopped fresh chives

Served still warm, this salad made with very waxy new potatoes is very good with a smoked sausage such as frankfurters.

Cook the potatoes in their skins, drain, peel, and cut them into thick slices. Pour over the oil and vinegar. Add plenty of salt and black pepper and 3 tablespoons chopped chives, and mix together lightly. Turn the salad into a serving dish and scatter the remaining chives over the top.

Kitchen Garden Salad

4 handfuls of mixed young green
   leaves (lettuce, summer spinach,
   sorrel, dandelion, mustard, etc.)
black pepper
pinch sugar
1 tablespoon lemon juice
3 tablespoons sunflower oil

This salad is for people who grow a good variety of leaf vegetables. It has a delicate flavor and is best served on its own as a first course or after the main dish.

Wash the leaves and shake them dry in a cloth or a salad spinner. Try not to bruise them. Pile them into a salad bowl. In another bowl, whisk together the pepper, sugar, lemon juice, and oil. Pour the dressing over the salad and toss gently. Serve immediately.

Cucumber and Cider Salad

2 cucumbers, peeled
5 fluid ounces dry cider
3 tablespoons chopped parsley
1 teaspoon sugar
salt and black pepper to taste

A very cool and refreshing salad whose pale green color looks very inviting on a hot day. It looks best in a glass bowl.

Cut the cucumbers in half lengthwise and scoop out the seeds with a spoon; discard the seeds. Slice the flesh thinly and put into a pretty glass bowl.

Mix together the cider, parsley, sugar, and seasoning. Pour this over the cucumber and chill for at least 1 hour. Toss gently just before serving.

Carrot and Red Currant Salad

1 pound carrots, scrubbed and
    coarsely grated
4 ounces red currants, removed
    from their stalks
1 tablespoon red currant jelly
2 tablespoons lemon juice

The rather tart red currants are excellent with carrots and they make a refreshing salad with an unusual color combination.

Combine the carrots and red currants and mix well together. Stir the red currant jelly into the lemon juice. Toss the salad in this mixture; then set it aside in the refrigerator to chill before serving.

Carrot and Apple Salad

1 pound carrots, scrubbed and
    coarsely grated
2 medium-sized, tart eating apples
    (1½ apples cored and finely
    chopped, ½ apple thinly sliced)
1 ounce sultana raisins, soaked
    for one hour in 1 tablespoon
    lemon juice
2 teaspoons French mustard
2 tablespoons olive oil
salt and black pepper to taste

Carrots and apples partner each other very well. Do not peel either the summer carrots or the apples, since most of the vitamins in both are contained in the skin or just beneath it. Do, however, remember to wash both well in case they have been sprayed.

Combine the carrot, chopped apple, raisins (reserving 1 teaspoon), and lemon juice in a serving bowl and mix well together. Beat the oil into the mustard and pour the mixture over the salad. Add salt and black pepper to taste.

Toss the salad well, garnish with the apple rings, and sprinkle the reserved raisins over the top.

Gingered Carrot Salad

1 pound carrots, scrubbed and
  finely grated
1 walnut-sized piece of fresh
  ginger
1 small clove garlic, crushed
4 tablespoons lemon juice
salt and black pepper

Grated carrot is such a good foil for so many flavors. This is a simple salad with an exotic touch.

Place the grated carrot in a fair-sized mixing bowl and grate the fresh ginger evenly across the surface. Beat the crushed garlic and the lemon juice together in a cup and pour it over the carrot and ginger. Season with salt and pepper and gently mix them together. Taste and adjust the seasoning, and then turn the salad onto a serving dish.

Tomatoes with Basil

1 pound tomatoes, cut lengthwise
  into six
1 medium onion, finely chopped
6–8 leaves basil, lightly chopped
salt and pepper to taste
1 tablespoon olive oil
1 teaspoon vinegar
heart of 1 small Romaine lettuce
2 teaspoons walnut oil
black olives to garnish

No herb has a greater affinity (or is it love?) for a vegetable (or is it a fruit?) than basil for tomato. Given ideal conditions, we would use fleshy Italian plum tomatoes, broad-leaved sweet basil, mild Spanish onions, and the tiny, flavorful Paris White Romaine lettuce which can be homegrown or bought in certain stores. We would never grow tired of this salad even if we had to eat it every day.

Place the tomatoes, onion, and basil in a mixing bowl. Season to taste with salt and pepper. Toss lightly together and pile in the center of a large, decorative serving plate.

Dribble the olive oil and the vinegar over the salad. Casually ring the central salad with the separated lettuce leaves. Dribble the walnut oil over the lettuce and garnish the whole salad with a scattering of black olives.

Mexican Cucumber

1 cucumber, peeled and finely
    diced
2 teaspoons salt
1 large clove garlic, crushed
2 tablespoons lime or lemon juice
1–2 red jalapeño peppers,
    deseeded and cut into paper-
    thin rings
sour cream for garnish

Toward the end of summer and in early autumn several of our growers have long 8-inch, hot, piquant red peppers for sale. The red jalapeño peppers, with their unmatchable, nose-twitching, hot peppery smell are also available at this time. You must not underestimate them. Either sort will enliven a simple cucumber salad.

If you want a lighter, low-fat topping, replace the sour cream with Strained Yogurt (page 128).

Place the cucumber in a colander, sprinkle with salt, and leave to drain for at least 30 minutes. Shake the cucumber free of all excess liquid and turn it into a small mixing bowl.

Add crushed garlic, citrus juice, and pepper rings. Mix well and arrange on four small plates. Put a good dollop of sour cream on each plate and serve.

Four-Color Salad with Japanese White Dressing

4 ounces white radish (daikon),
    peeled and cut into match-
    sticks
4 ounces carrots, peeled, cut
    into thin rounds
4 ounces green beans, topped,
    tailed (string if needed)
2 ounces dried apricots, washed
    and finely chopped
Japanese White Dressing,
    vinegared variation (page 140)

A Japanese-inspired salad that combines different colors, shapes, tastes, and textures in a delicious and healthy way. Serve as a starter or as an accompaniment to a main meal. This is particularly good with spiced and/or chili hot dishes when its cooling, sweetish flavor is much appreciated.

Parboil the radish and carrots in lightly salted boiling water for just 2 minutes. Drain and rinse immediately in cold water, and drain again. Parboil the beans for 3 minutes. Drain and chill in cold water; drain again. Combine the vegetables and dried apricots and stir in the white dressing. Serve on individual plates.

oil for deep frying
1¼ pounds green beans, topped
    and tailed
1 tablespoon vegetable oil
2 teaspoons chopped ginger root
2 tablespoons water or stock
1 teaspoon salt
1 teaspoon sugar
2 teaspoons tamari
1 teaspoon vinegar
1 teaspoon sesame oil
2-3 spring onions, finely sliced

A dainty Chinese-inspired salad whose unusual flavor and texture are achieved by deep frying the beans in oil (like French fries). The beans can also be stir-fried in a sauté pan or wok.

Heat the frying oil in a deep pan. Gently place the washed and well-dried beans in a deep-frying basket and lower into the oil. Remove the beans after 3-4 minutes when the skins have begun to blister. Drain the beans. Reheat the oil to very hot and replace the beans. Cook for 1 or 2 minutes until they have started to turn crisp and brown. Remove the beans and leave to drain again on paper towels to remove excess oil.

Heat the vegetable oil over a medium heat in a small frying pan (but one which will hold the beans), add half the chopped ginger, and cook for no more than 1 minute, stirring constantly. Add the stock, salt, and sugar and reduce by one-third, still stirring constantly. Add the drained beans before the contents of the frying pan begin to brown, and then, still stirring, cook off all the liquid.

Empty the contents of the frying pan into a serving dish. Add the tamari, vinegar, and sesame oil and mix well. Garnish with the remaining chopped ginger and the sliced onions and chill well before serving.

Tabouli

8 ounces fine bulgur (cracked
 wheat)

8 ounces onion and/or spring
 onion, finely chopped

2 bunches fresh parsley, chopped

4 tablespoons chopped fresh
 mint or 4 teaspoons crushed
 dried mint

3 medium tomatoes, finely
 chopped

4 fluid ounces lemon juice

4 fluid ounces olive oil

1 teaspoon allspice (optional)

salt and black pepper to taste

wedges of lemon for garnish

This recipe is adapted from one in David Scott's book, Traditional
Arab Cookery. *Tabouli is a Middle Eastern salad made with bulgur
(cracked wheat), lots of fresh parsley and mint, lemon juice, and olive
oil. There are no hard and fast rules and the way the salad is prepared depends very much on individual taste.*

*The recipe given here is a guide and you should vary the amounts
used to suit yourself. Tabouli can be served as a starter, side salad,
or main-dish salad. It's also very good as a filling in pita bread
with falafel (Middle Eastern deep fried bean croquettes) or kebabs.*

Cover the bulgur with plenty of cold water and leave for 1 hour.
Drain in a colander and squeeze out any excess water by gently
pressing the wheat with your hand (or patting dry in a clean dishtowel). Put the bulgur into a large serving bowl and gently stir in all
the remaining ingredients except the lemon wedges. Taste, and adjust
the seasoning. Garnish with lemon wedges.

1 pound cold boiled potatoes,
   finely diced
4 ounces tomatoes, finely diced
2 medium-sized eating apples,
   cored and finely diced
1 medium-sized onion
salt to taste
2 tablespoons Hot Sweet and Sour
   Mango Cilantro Dressing
   (page 134)
4 crisp papadoms, or 4 crisply
   fried Indian puris, or fried
   Mexican flour tortillas, lightly
   crushed (optional)
2 ounces puffed rice or Rice
   Krispies (optional)
2 ounces lightly broken potato
   chips (optional)
juice of 1 large lemon
lightly chopped cilantro leaves
   to garnish

Short eats are pungent or sweet snacks of Sri Lankan/Indian origin. They go well with a few drinks or a beer (not, we hasten to add, with fine wines). Do find some excuse to try this salad—it's ideal party food. Spoon out onto very small plates or shallow dishes and eat with a teaspoon before the papadoms or puffed rice have gone soft.

The papadoms (crisp Indian bread), puffed rice, and potato chips are all optional in that they don't alter the taste of the dish. It is still well worth doing without them, but then you miss out on all the different textures and half the fun.

Put the potatoes, tomatoes, apples, and onions into a mixing bowl, and season to taste with salt. Stir in the dressing and mix well. Fold in the papadoms, puffed rice, and potato chips. Pile the mixture onto a serving dish. Dress with lemon juice and garnish with chopped cilantro.

2 medium-sized eggplants
(1–1¼ pounds)
2 teaspoons salt
3 tablespoons tamari
2 tablespoons wine vinegar
1 tablespoon sesame oil
1 tablespoon sugar
1 tablespoon neutral oil for frying
(e.g., sunflower seed oil)
1 large green pepper, cut in
medium-sized rings
1 walnut-sized piece of fresh
ginger, peeled and grated
4 cloves garlic, chopped finely
salt and hot pepper sauce or chili
paste to taste
1 tablespoon sesame seeds

This is Paddy's favorite eggplant dish. It's a cooked salad, so takes a little longer to prepare, but it's well worth the effort.

Cut the eggplants in half, salt and drain them, and then steam them for at least half an hour until they are soft and collapsed. Drain well and set aside. If you have no special steamer, put the eggplants in a small metal colander or sieve placed inside a large covered saucepan partly filled with water.

Meanwhile, whisk together the tamari, wine vinegar, sesame oil, and sugar, and set aside. Heat the oil in a frying pan and lightly sauté the green pepper for 1–2 minutes over a medium heat (it should still be crunchy). Add the ginger and garlic and cook for not more than one minute (if the garlic burns it will become bitter and ruin the flavor), stirring constantly. Combine these together with the soy mixture in a saucepan and bring gently to a boil.

Remove from the heat. Dry-roast the sesame seeds in a heavy pan over medium heat until they begin to dance; remove them to a plate. Chop the eggplants into rough 1-inch cubes and place these in a serving bowl. Add the sauce and stir well. Allow to cool, chill, and sprinkle with the toasted sesame seeds before serving.

Ratatouille

12 ounces small eggplants, cut
   into ½-inch slices
12 ounces small zucchini, cut
   into ½-inch slices
salt
2 medium-sized onions, sliced
5 fluid ounces olive oil
2 medium-sized red or green
   peppers, stems and seeds
   removed, sliced
2–3 cloves garlic, finely sliced
1 pound ripe tomatoes, peeled,
   seeds and excess liquid
   squeezed out, and roughly
   chopped
sprig of thyme
1 tablespoon parsley, chopped
salt and pepper
10 torn basil leaves for
   garnish (optional)

Correctly cooked ratatouille is one of the most delicious and versatile of all vegetable dishes—it can be served hot as a vegetable or warm or cold as a salad. The vegetables should be just tender and bright-colored and the sauce thick. The use of at least two frying pans simplifies its preparation. It is essential to use olive oil and small firm eggplants and zucchini, and to rid the tomatoes of excess liquid.

Unless the eggplants and zucchini are very young and firm, salt them and leave them to stand for at least half an hour in a colander to drain the juices out. Rinse, then gently pat the slices dry on absorbent paper towels.

Cook the onions in 2 tablespoons of oil over a medium heat for 5 minutes until they begin to soften. Reduce the heat, add the peppers and the garlic and cook gently for a further 15 minutes, or until the vegetables are just tender. Set aside.

Place 2 tablespoons of oil in a saucepan over a brisk heat, add the tomatoes and quickly (2–3 minutes) reduce them to a thick pulp. Flavor the tomatoes with thyme, season with salt and pepper, and add them to the onions and peppers. Brown the zucchini slices for 6–8 minutes in another 2 tablespoons of oil in a frying pan over brisk heat, drain, and set aside. Brown the eggplant slices in a similar manner in the remaining oil, drain, and add these to the zucchini.

Combine all the cooked vegetables and the parsley in a casserole set on an extremely low heat. Stir them gently together and check the seasoning. The ratatouille is now ready to serve. It may be served warm, but it is at its best cold. If you have fresh basil available, tear it up and stir it in just before serving.

Indian Tomato Salad

1 pound firm tomatoes, quartered
1 small onion, finely diced
6 fluid ounces natural yogurt
pinch cayenne
½ teaspoon ground cumin
2 tablespoons finely chopped
   fresh mint
salt and black pepper to taste

A spicy, mint-flavored tomato salad usually served with curry dishes.

Combine the tomatoes and onion in a serving bowl. Stir together the yogurt, cayenne, cumin, and mint; add salt and black pepper to taste. Gently toss the ingredients in this dressing and serve.

Sweet Red Pepper Salad

3–4 firm red peppers, skinned
   and seeded
8 large firm black olives
1 clove garlic, crushed
2 tablespoons olive oil
1 tablespoon lemon or lime juice
salt and pepper to taste

This salad is beautiful to behold and has a taste to match. It has a rich, powerful flavor and is best served in small quantities. Try serving it as one of several salads and tidbits in an Italian-style antipasto or with a plain baked potato and a smothered lettuce salad for contrast.

Cut the peppers into ⅜-inch-wide strips and place in a small mixing bowl. Cut the olives in half and remove the pits. If the olives have tough skins, it is a simple and worthwhile task to peel these off.

Slice the olives into small crescents and add them and the remaining ingredients to the peppers. Mix gently but thoroughly, cover, and leave in a cool place for at least 2 hours for the flavors to develop. Adjust the seasoning before serving.

Cooked Pepper and Cheese Salad

2 large red peppers, washed and cut in half
2 large yellow peppers, washed and cut in half
4 fluid ounces olive oil
1 ounce Parmesan or strong cheddar cheese, grated
1 tablespoon dried breadcrumbs
2 tablespoons capers
1 tablespoon chopped fresh mint or marjoram
1 teaspoon wine vinegar
sea salt to taste

A bright orange-red and yellow salad dotted with green. Serve as a first course.

To remove the skin from the peppers, preheat the broiler to 325° and place them, rounded side up, in the broiler pan. Cook for a few minutes until the skins are charred; remove from the heat and peel off the skins. Cut peppers in half again and deseed them.

Heat the olive oil in a frying pan and fry the peppers gently for 5 minutes on each side.

Arrange the peppers in a serving dish, alternating red and yellow to achieve a spoked effect. Whisk the grated cheese with the bread crumbs and sprinkle the mixture over the peppers. Sprinkle the mint or marjoram over the capers, and add a few grindings of sea salt. Leave to cool slightly, then pour over the vinegar. Serve immediately, or cool and serve chilled.

Fresh Mint and Apple Salad

3 medium eating apples, cored and diced
4 tablespoons chopped fresh mint
10 fluid ounces natural yogurt
1 tablespoon clear honey

This salad is particularly refreshing on a hot summer's day and it is also a good accompaniment to hot spicy meals like curries. Try it with early apples such as Vistabella, Paula Reds, or Tydeman Reds, or in late summer use McIntosh or Cortland. The last oxidizes slowly, so it keeps a good white color when cut.

Combine the apples and mint in a serving bowl and add the yogurt and honey. Mix well together; chill before serving.

Autumn Salads

Early autumn offers the salad maker a veritable cornucopia of local produce at a very reasonable price. Nearly all of the native-grown summer vegetables are still available, although the season lacks the excitement of newly arrived vegetables. Abundant apples, pears, and grapes are supplemented by fresh figs, dates, pomegranates, and the beginning of the main Florida crop of avocados.

This happy situation rapidly changes. Vegetables cease growing so quickly, become tougher and more fibrous and lose their sweetness as the strength of the sun wanes. The exception to this are mature sweet red peppers and chilies which achieve a rich mellowness not to be had at other times of the year. Autumn winds and damp cause further deterioration, and annual plants die back, leaving only the hardy spinach, chicory, celery, fennel, drumhead cabbages, and the root crops. It is time to begin buying southern vegetables again.

EARLY AUTUMN

Local bush and pole beans are still available, but take care they are not overmature, fibrous, and full of starch. Look out for and buy the semi-dried shell beans, preferably those still in their pods. Sweet corn is still available, but only worth buying if the husk is still a fresh green and the kernels a pale yellow. Zucchinis are still obtainable, but slice and salt them to remove the slight bitter taste they often have at this time of the year. If you have grown sweet basil, strip the plants and preserve the leaves in jars in olive oil, or make a pesto sauce.

MID- AND LATE AUTUMN

All root crops, brassicas, celery, and watercress are in fine condition. Chinese cabbage is now at its best. Look out for bulb fennel and chicories of all types. Belgian endive is now much more reasonably priced. Cucumbers, tomatoes, and beans will now be coming to us primarily from Florida and California. As the more colorful vegetables end their season, enliven your salads with fresh dates, kiwifruit, pomegranates, and avocados. If you have a cool, airy place to store them, buy a bag of shallots. They have many uses, not only in salads, and will keep well into spring.

Pear, Grape, and Cucumber Salad

SERVES 4 TO 6

3 ripe but firm sweet pears, peeled and cored—one thinly sliced, the rest diced
½ medium cucumber, divided in half lengthwise, seeds scooped out (slice ¼ cucumber, dice the rest)
4 ounces black or green seedless grapes, washed
Vinaigrette Dressing (page 125)

A simple, yet unusual combination, which makes a good side salad for a dish with cheese in it or simply as an accompaniment to cheese and bread. Served well chilled, it also makes an appetizing starter. Try it with the new-season pears available from midsummer onward. Black grapes are the most impressive with this salad but they should be used only when you have time to seed them.

Small, green, seedless grapes are available very cheaply starting in summer.

Make a bed of the pear and cucumber slices in a small salad bowl. Put the remaining pear, cucumber, and grapes (reserve 5 or 6 grapes) into a bowl and toss them in vinaigrette dressing to taste. Pour this mixture over the bed of pear and cucumber slices. Garnish the salad with the reserved grapes, chill, and serve.

3–4 firm, sweet red peppers,
  skinned and deseeded
5 fluid ounces Raw Tomato Sauce
  (page 129), chilled
3 fluid ounces whipping cream,
  chilled
pepper and salt (optional)
1 teaspoon chopped parsley
  to garnish

This salad is rich and beautiful: green, red and white flotsam in a sea of red. Serve in small portions.

Slice the red peppers into ¼-inch rings. Place them in a small bowl, add the sauce and the cream, and gently stir together. Season the salad, if necessary. Garnish with the chopped parsley and serve immediately.

VARIATION

Remove the center core and seeds of 4 large tomatoes. Grill them lightly, skin side up, under a hot broiler. Now, turn the tomatoes skin side down, season them, and repeat the broiling process. Set the tomatoes aside on four small individual plates and stuff them full to overflowing with the pepper and tomato cream salad. Add an extra teaspoon of cream to each tomato, and serve.

Spice Street Salad

8 ounces cauliflower florets

8 ounces fresh young carrots, scrubbed, topped and tailed, and cut into thin rounds

8 ounces green beans, topped and tailed

2 tablespoons olive oil

3–4 tablespoons Spicy Almond Dressing (page 137)

It is strange how we in the West have until recently used heavy spices only for pickling vinegars and for smothering any unwelcome taints that may be lurking in preserved or not-so-well-preserved meats. In the Middle East spice mixtures of all different sorts are bought in little paper cones which one dips bread into or scatters over dishes just as we use salt and pepper.

Here we use one of these mixtures on the freshest of summer vegetables which have been lightly cooked and then quickly cooled to safeguard their color and texture.

This salad is ruined if the vegetables are overcooked, so steam them together for just 3–4 minutes and cook them individually in a small amount of boiling salted water for the same length of time. Whichever cooking method you use, as soon as they are cooked, plunge them under cold running water until they are quite cold.

Toss the vegetables in a mixing bowl, add the olive oil, and mix well. Turn the salad onto a serving dish and sprinkle with the Spicy Almond Dressing.

Paprika Potatoes

1¼ pounds potatoes, peeled and
cooked, though still firm
half a medium-sized onion,
diced small
1 large sweet red pepper, seeded
and finely diced
3 fluid ounces Mayonnaise
(page 126)
3 fluid ounces natural yogurt or
sour cream
2 teaspoons paprika
pinch caraway seeds
salt to taste
chopped parsley to garnish

A hearty, robust, but good-looking salad, since the red and green garnish is very pretty. It makes good use of those tasty, mellow red peppers available in autumn. At this time of the year we would probably use small Katahdin, Sebago, or Centennial potatoes.

Cut the potatoes into bite-sized pieces and turn them into a large mixing bowl. Add the diced onion and all but 1 tablespoon of the diced red pepper. Add all the remaining ingredients except the parsley and stir well.

Taste, adjust the seasoning, and turn onto a serving dish. Garnish with the reserved diced red pepper and the parsley.

Sweet and Sour Celery and Apple Salad

2 medium-sized eating apples,
cored and diced
2 stalks celery, finely chopped
2 tablespoons lemon juice
1 tablespoon clear honey
1 ounce chopped walnuts

The salad is lightly dressed in a sweet and sour mixture of honey and lemon juice, and it is at its best with matching sweet-sour apples like the Paula Reds, which are available in late summer and autumn.

Combine the apple and celery in a serving bowl. Pour over them the lemon juice and honey, mix well together, and chill before serving sprinkled with chopped walnuts.

VARIATION

Replace the lemon juice with double the quantity of natural yogurt.

Tomato, Apple, and Watercress Salad

1 bunch watercress, coarsely
   shredded
½ medium cooking apple, or
   1 eating apple, cored and
   chopped
1 tablespoon lemon juice
salt and black pepper to taste
8 ounces firm tomatoes, sliced
4 fluid ounces Mayonnaise
   (page 126)

*A simple but colorful late summer, autumn, or winter salad
which makes a good starter or side salad. For a late summer salad
try Cortland apples, for autumn, Stayman-Winesap and in the winter
months, Red Delicious.*

Combine the watercress with the apples, toss the mixture in the
lemon juice, and season it with salt and black pepper. Arrange the
tomatoes in the bottom of a serving bowl and salt and pepper them
to taste.

Pile the apple and watercress on top and serve the salad with a
separate bowl of mayonnaise.

Apple and Celery with Almond and Tahini Dressing

9 ounces crisp apples, well washed
Vinaigrette Dressing (page 125)
½ head celery (9 ounces),
   trimmed and washed
2 tablespoons tahini sauce
4 fluid ounces natural yogurt
salt and pepper to taste
2 ounces flaked almonds

*A light, modern version of the maître d's famous creation at the
Waldorf Astoria. He was fond of saying "my job is the serving of food,
never the cooking." Maybe his head chef should have said, "I think
that salad would be better done this way."*

Core the apples and cut them into small chunks, dropping them
immediately into the French dressing to prevent them from discoloring.
Cut the celery sticks into ⅜-inch sections and place them in a mixing
bowl. Add the tahini and yogurt, mix well, and season to taste with
salt and pepper. Thoroughly drain the apple chunks (you can use the
remaining dressing another time), add them to the dressed celery,
and again mix well. Fold in most of the flaked almonds and turn the
salad into a serving dish, decorating the top with a few reserved
almonds.

Cucumber, Kiwifruit, and Pomegranate Salad

8-inch length of cucumber, peeled
salt
4 kiwifruit, peeled
1 pomegranate

A beautiful-looking, refreshing starter salad. It is served plain— any vinegar or citrus-based dressing would quite destroy the subtle flavor of the kiwifruit. The sweet pomegranate juice, with that slightly bitter aftertang, is enough to enhance this delicate salad.

Finely slice the peeled cucumber, lightly sprinkle the rounds with salt, and leave, lightly pressed, for at least 30 minutes. Drain off any liquid.

Finely slice the kiwifruit in a manner similar to the cucumber. Decorate four small plain side plates in a spiral pattern, alternating cucumber rounds with kiwifruit rounds. Loosely overlap the slices so that the beautiful center of the kiwifruit is not obscured. Cut the pomegranate in half laterally, pull the fruit apart, and scatter the seeds across each individual salad, taking care not to include any bitter yellow skin.

Green Bean and Tomato Salad

9 ounces green beans, topped
   and tailed
1 pound tomatoes, sliced
4 shallots, finely sliced
1 large clove garlic, very finely
   sliced
3 fluid ounces Vinaigrette
   Dressing (page 125)
salt and black pepper to taste

In autumn, most of our green beans come from Florida, and the rest, from other southern states and Mexico. We prefer to use shallots with the beans and tomatoes. You never need many of them and their attractive, pungent flavor is well worth the extra cost over that of frequently bitter onions.

Drop the beans into a pan of rapidly boiling salted water and cook uncovered for 5–8 minutes until just tender. Drain the beans and rapidly cool them under cold running water.

Combine all the ingredients and mix well. Set the salad aside for an hour in a cool place to allow the flavors to mingle. Adjust the seasoning and serve.

Navy Bean Salad

8 ounces dried navy beans,
   soaked overnight
4 sticks of celery, washed and
   finely sliced
2 tablespoons chopped spring
   onion
salt and pepper to taste
5 fluid ounces Green Dressing
   (page 128)
sprigs of watercress for garnish

This salad is obviously best made with navy beans picked directly from the semi-dried pods. Look out for these beans in early autumn. You can substitute French horticultural beans.

For a treat, serve the salad piled in the center of halves of small Persian or Crenshaw melons.

Drain the beans and cook them in fresh unsalted water until they are tender (about 1–1½ hours). Drain the beans and set them aside to cool.

Combine the beans in a mixing bowl with the celery and onion and season well with salt and pepper. Finally, stir in the Green Dressing, turn the salad into a serving bowl, and garnish with the sprigs of watercress.

Cauliflower Salad

1 small cauliflower, cleaned
salt
4 tablespoons olive oil
1 clove garlic, crushed
pinch of cayenne
½ teaspoon French mustard
black pepper to taste
4 canned anchovies, chopped,
   or 7 or 8 black olives

For this salad, the cauliflower is parboiled and should remain firm and still crisp. It is tossed in a hot dressing before chilling to ensure that the cauliflower absorbs the full flavor of the dressing. The finished salad is garnished with chopped anchovies or olives before serving.

Choose a pan big enough to hold the whole cauliflower. Add 1 inch salted water. Cover and boil the cauliflower for 6 to 7 minutes. Drain it and run it under cold water until it is cool enough to handle. Cut the cauliflower into small florets and put them into a serving bowl.

Combine the oil, lemon juice, garlic, cayenne, mustard, and seasoning to taste in a small pan and bring the mixture to a boil. Whisk it well together and pour it over the cauliflower. Toss well and set the salad in the refrigerator to chill. Just before serving, garnish the top with chopped anchovies or black olives.

Tomatoes in Hot Green Tomato Sauce

6 medium-sized ripe tomatoes
2 spring onions, complete with
   green leaves
1 medium green or partially
   green tomato
1 tablespoon fresh, coarsely
   chopped parsley
1 tablespoon cottage cheese
1 clove garlic
¼ small fresh or dried red chili
   pepper or ¼ teaspoon chili
   sauce
salt and black pepper to taste

At the beginning and end of the local tomato growing season there are lots of green and partly green tomatoes available. They often go to waste, because we have been conditioned to eat tomatoes only when they are red. This is a shame, as the hard fruit usually has the best flavor. With this recipe, you get the best of both worlds.

Quarter the ripe tomatoes and set them aside. Wash and trim the spring onions, removing any damaged leaves. Chop them roughly and place them in a blender or food processor. Quarter the green tomato and add that and the remaining ingredients to the blender.

Blend for a few seconds at high speed. Test and adjust the seasoning. Pour the dressing over the reserved quartered tomatoes, and mix well.

Chinese Cabbage and Pomegranate in Poppy Seed Dressing

18 ounces Chinese cabbage
   (about half a large one),
   trimmed
1 pomegranate
5 fluid ounces Poppy Seed
   Dressing (page 134)

While the pomegranate is not essential to this salad, its soft pink or red seeds make a lovely color contrast with the crisp, pale green cabbage leaves. They also give an added dimension to the sweet-sharp dressing. This makes a delicious alternative to a green salad.

Wash the Chinese cabbage well, shake dry, and remove any discolored leaves. Slice the leaves across into ⅜-inch sections and place these in a large mixing bowl. Cut the pomegranate across laterally and break out the seeds over the cabbage, taking care not to include any bitter yellow skin.

Pour the Poppy Seed Dressing over all and toss well. Turn into a serving dish.

Bean Sprout and Cucumber Salad

8 ounces bean sprouts, washed
   and drained
1½ medium cucumbers, sliced in
   half lengthwise, seeded and
   cut into matchsticks
2 tablespoons finely diced
   spring onion
3 fluid ounces cider vinegar
1 tablespoon white sugar
½ teaspoon salt

This is a very simple but effective Indonesian salad. It contains no fat, but the dressing is quite sweet. Replace the sugar with clear honey if you prefer its flavor. For a more robust dish, toss the finished salad with a handful of roasted unsalted peanuts.

Combine the bean sprouts, cucumber, and onion. Stir the vinegar, sugar, and salt together until the sugar dissolves. Toss the salad in this dressing and serve.

Cheese Salad with Lime and Yogurt Dressing

8 ounces Cheddar, Gruyère, or
   Emmenthal cheese cut into
   1½-inch cubes
1 large green pepper, seeded
   and chopped
2 medium-sized tomatoes,
   quartered
4 fluid ounces natural yogurt
juice of 1 lime
½ teaspoon French mustard
small pinch cayenne pepper
½ teaspoon dried basil

An unusual salad, which is very good served with olives, a green salad, and crusty French bread. If limes are unavailable, use lemon juice.

Combine the cheese with the pepper and tomatoes. Beat together the yogurt, lime juice, mustard, cayenne, and basil. Stir this mixture into the cheese salad. Chill and serve.

Moroccan Cooked Salad

2 medium-sized tomatoes,
   quartered
2 medium-sized onions, coarsely
   diced
½ cucumber, sliced in half
   lengthwise, seeded and sliced
   in rings
1 sweet red or green pepper,
   seeded and chopped
4 tablespoons water
3 tablespoons olive oil
2 tablespoons lemon juice
2 cloves garlic, crushed
salt and black pepper to taste
2 tablespoons chopped fresh
   cilantro leaves

Cooked salads are a great favorite in North Africa, where they are served as a side dish to a main meal. They keep well and improve the day after preparation. Fresh cilantro is essential for this salad.

Put the tomatoes, onion, cucumber, green pepper, and water into a pan, simmer for 4 to 5 minutes and then set aside.

Beat together the oil, lemon juice, garlic, and salt and black pepper. Strain any liquid from the vegetables in the pan and then pour in the dressing. Add the chopped cilantro and gently mix. Transfer the salad to a serving bowl and serve at room temperature.

Cottage Cheese Salad

8 ounces cottage cheese
1 firm eating apple, cored and
    chopped
1 firm, ripe pear, cored and
    chopped
1 tablespoon roasted unsalted
    peanuts (or other nuts)
2 teaspoons poppy seeds
1 tablespoon lemon juice
1 teaspoon clear honey (optional)
salt and black pepper to taste

Cottage cheese is nutritious and very low in fat, and this salad served with brown bread makes a healthy and enjoyable light meal.
Other fresh fruit, depending on what is in season, may be used in this salad. We recommend seedless green grapes, apricots, peaches, pineapple, and melon.

Combine all the ingredients, mix well, and serve.

Celery and Banana Salad

½ head celery, washed, cut into
    ½-inch sections
3–4 firm bananas, peeled and cut
    into ½-inch rounds
2 tablespoons cumin seeds
1 teaspoon coriander seeds
1 teaspoon cardamom pods
7 fluid ounces natural yogurt
salt and cayenne pepper to taste

Like many a couple, celery and banana make a good marriage because they have such different characteristics. The celery, crisp and slightly salty, is set against the soft, slightly sweet banana. Dressed up with a light, spicy sauce, they make an unusual but extremely tasty dish.

Put the celery and the banana in a mixing bowl. Lightly toast the cumin and coriander seeds in a heavy metal pan until they begin to dance. Empty the seeds into a mortar, add the cardamom, and grind lightly. Remove the cardamom husks, then add the spices to the yogurt in a small bowl. Season the yogurt with the salt and cayenne pepper and stir well. Add the spiced yogurt to the celery and banana and fold gently together. Turn into a serving bowl and serve.

4 tablespoons olive oil
1 teaspoon coriander seeds,
freshly ground
1 bay leaf
9 ounces white button
mushrooms, stems trimmed
2 teaspoons lemon juice
salt and pepper to taste
bay leaves and lemon portions
to garnish

This elegant salad has become something of a modern classic. It is simple to prepare, but do please note the following points. The rich aromatic flavor of olive oil is essential to this salad, so don't substitute any other. We have had the mushrooms served to us awash in a weak flavored juice: avoid this by cooking the mushrooms, uncovered, in a small frying pan or sauté pan (not a high-sided saucepan). Preferably, use small button mushrooms; failing these, larger ones, halved or quartered, will do fine. Whichever type you choose, they must be very fresh.

Heat the olive oil in a sauté pan over medium heat. Add the ground coriander and the bay leaf to the hot oil. As soon as the bay leaf starts to darken, tip in the mushrooms and add the lemon juice.

Season with salt and pepper and cook, stirring frequently, for 3–4 minutes or until the mushrooms have a translucent look about them (achieved when the hot oil has penetrated the center). Adjust seasoning, allow to cool, place in serving dish or dishes, and chill. Garnish with bay leaves and lemon sections before serving.

Humus bi Tabini

SERVES 6 TO 8

**8 ounces chick-peas, well
   washed, checked for small
   stones, soaked overnight
1 fluid ounce vegetable oil
2–3 cloves garlic
2 tablespoons white vinegar
juice of 2 lemons
5 fluid ounces tahini
up to 1 teaspoon salt and up to
   ½ teaspoon pepper
paprika and oil to garnish
pita bread to serve**

One wonders what it is that makes humus the favorite small salad of the Middle East. The name is odd, it looks rather plain, the ingredients are unexciting, and yet it is popular enough to be found in delis the length and breadth of this country. It must be the taste that gives it such appeal, and yet even this is not obvious at first. You dip in your piece of bread, scoop up some humus, and pop it into your mouth. Not bad, you think, and you try some more. You quickly discover that it is quite compulsive, addictive even, and you try more and more and more. That is why in our restaurant we sell gallons of humus every week. Our recipe is different from the normal ethnic versions, but a great many people have said how much they prefer ours.

Drain the chick-peas, cover again with unsalted water, and simmer, covered, for about 2 hours, or until the chick-peas offer no resistance when squeezed between finger and thumb (add more water during cooking if necessary). Drain, reserving the liquid.

Set aside about 24 chick-peas. Pour the rest into a small mixing bowl, add the vegetable oil, garlic, wine vinegar, and lemon juice, and mix well. Pour this mixture into a blender and blend at high speed until smooth. If the mixture is too stiff to blend, dilute with a little of the reserved cooking liquid. Return the mixture to the mixing bowl, add the tahini and seasoning, and mix well.

Spoon onto individual plates. Make a small depression in the center of each salad, dribble in the oil, and garnish with the reserved chick-peas and a sprinkling of paprika. Serve with hot pita bread.

Apple and Grapes with Japanese Mustard Dressing

8 ounces eating apples, cored,
  cut into small chunks
juice of ½ lemon
8 ounces large grapes, washed
2 tablespoons Japanese Mustard
  Dressing (page 138)
1 teaspoon mustard seeds

The large black Ribier grapes available in early winter and around Christmas are excellent with this salad, which makes an unusual, bittersweet appetizer.

The seedless variety of red Tokay grapes could also be used in this recipe.

Sprinkle the apple with lemon juice and set aside to chill. Cut the grapes in half and pick out the seeds with the tip of a pointed knife. Lightly chill the grapes. Toss the apple and grapes in the dressing and garnish with the mustard seeds. Serve in bowls.

Tomato and Green Bean Salad

8 ounces green beans, fresh or
  frozen, topped and tailed
1 pound firm tomatoes, quartered
2 tablespoons freshly chopped
  parsley
5 ounces natural yogurt
1 tablespoon tahini
1 tablespoon lemon juice
½ clove garlic, crushed
salt and black pepper to taste

Sometimes in the winter and spring tomatoes are not very tasty, and in this salad we have used a strongly flavored yogurt and tahini dressing to compensate. With its bright reds and greens this is a colorful salad and, with the dressing, nutritious as well.

Cook the green beans in rapidly boiling salted water for about 7 or 8 minutes or until *al dente* or firm to the bite. (If using frozen beans, cook according to the instructions on the packet.) Cool them rapidly under cold running water to retain the color and texture. Mix the beans with the tomatoes and most of the parsley (reserve a little for garnishing).

Combine the tahini, lemon juice, garlic, salt, and black pepper and stir the mixture into the salad until the beans and tomatoes are well coated. Transfer the salad to a serving dish, garnish it with reserved parsley, and serve at once.

Fruit and Vegetable Yogurt Salad

SERVES 4 TO 6

2 medium-sized eating apples,
   cored and chopped
2 medium-sized carrots, peeled,
   thinly sliced
1 medium-sized green pepper,
   seeded and chopped
6 ounces fresh or canned
   pineapple pieces
6 fluid ounces natural yogurt
3 tablespoons orange juice
1 tablespoon lemon juice
pinch of salt
cinnamon to garnish

This salad is a versatile side dish which can be served with many types of main-course meals; its sweet refreshing flavor contrasts especially well with hot spicy dishes.

Combine the apples, carrots, peppers, and pineapple and mix well. Stir together the yogurt, orange and lemon juices, and salt. Toss the salad in this dressing, chill, and serve with cinnamon dusted over the top.

Spinach with Sesame Seed and Soy Dressing

1 pound spinach
salt
4 tablespoons Sesame Seed and
   Soy Dressing (page 141)

Wash the spinach leav   vell. Bring a large pan of lightly salted water to a boil. Add the spinach and cook very briefly. As soon as the spinach droops, quickly drain it and rinse under cold water until cooled. Drain it well again and gently squeeze out excess water. Chop the spinach into about 1½-inch lengths. Toss the spinach in the dressing and serve in deep individual serving bowls.

SERVES 4 OR MORE

Mezze *are Middle Eastern hors d'oeuvres. They may be hot or cold, complicated and exotic or simple and quick to prepare, but they are always delicious. Here is a selection of ideas for readily available, easily made salad* mezze. *Choose three or four and arrange them on individual plates, one per diner. Consider contrasts in color, texture, and taste when making your choice. Serve the* mezze *with wedges of lemon and a small bowl of lightly salted natural yogurt. No fixed amounts have been given since the amount you prepare of each* mezze *will depend on how many guests you have and how many* mezze *you wish to put on each plate. They should look delicious and tempting but shouldn't be filling, just appetizing.*

- Black or green olives in a lemon-and-oil dressing.
- Thin slices of cucumber lightly sprinkled with fresh mint.
- Slices of hard-boiled egg, dusted with ground cinnamon, ground coriander, and salt.
- Cottage cheese mixed with a little tahini and sprinkled with cumin seeds.
- Fresh, crunchy radishes straight from the refrigerator, with two or three leaves left on.
- Cubes of avocado with vinaigrette dressing, garnished with thin slices of orange.
- Almonds in their skins, sprinkled with salty water and baked in the oven until browned.
- Green beans, lightly cooked, rinsed under cold water until cooled, drained, and dressed in lemon juice and oil.
- Fresh or dried dates stuffed with sour cream.

Mixed-Up Bean Sprout Salad

8 ounces bean sprouts, washed
and drained
4 ounces canned water chestnuts,
drained and sliced
4 ounces fresh (or canned,
drained) pineapple cubes
¼ teaspoon ground cumin
¼ teaspoon ground coriander
1 teaspoon tamari
3 tablespoons Mayonnaise
(page 126) or Tofu Dressing
(page 132)
pinch ground coriander

This salad is called mixed-up because it has Chinese, Indian, and Indonesian origins, reflecting the culinary influences that have affected Southeast Asian cookery. Surprisingly, the mixed flavors work well and the salad is handy to make if you are short of fresh ingredients. For a low-fat salad use the Tofu Dressing rather than the mayonnaise.

Combine the bean sprouts, water chestnuts, and pineapple and mix well. Stir the cumin, coriander, and tamari into the mayonnaise or dressing and pour the mixture over the salad. Toss well, garnish with a pinch of ground coriander, and serve at once.

Ginger and Yogurt Rice Salad

1 pound cooked long-grain rice
1 medium-sized green pepper,
cored, seeded, finely chopped
1 stalk celery, finely chopped
2 ounces roasted almonds
walnut-sized piece of ginger root,
peeled and finely chopped
8 fluid ounces natural yogurt
salt to taste
paprika to taste

A filling, but quite refreshing, rice salad.

Combine the rice with the pepper, celery and nuts. Stir the ginger into the yogurt and add the mixture to the rice, with salt to taste. Set aside for about 1 hour in the refrigerator to allow the ginger flavor to permeate the salad. Garnish with a pinch of paprika and serve.

Winter Salads

Winter is a time of little change—the same foods are available all season. There is still plenty of choice, although now is the time to make judicious use of the pantry shelf. Dried beans, cooked pasta, canned tomatoes, sweet corn, and so on will be used to make hearty nutritious salads. We will be looking at salads that stimulate the appetite for warming meals, and at salads eaten at the end of a meal to leave the palate feeling fresh and clean.

Side salads eaten as a counterpoint to a robust main course are also important. Sometimes, too, we will want to introduce the cheerful colors and crisp textures of vegetables and fruit grown in southern climates. We will show you that creating tasty salads in winter is simple, provided you avoid those varieties that are only at their best in the summer. And do not overlook salads as a valuable source of vitamins, minerals, fiber, and high-quality protein in our winter diet.

VEGETABLES TO LOOK FOR

Potatoes, carrots, red and white cabbage, Brussels sprouts, turnips, celery, broccoli, cauliflower, onions, lettuce, and leeks are dependable winter vegetables. Look for some of the less common treats from warmer climates, such as tomatoes, zucchini, green beans, and snow peas (from Mexico); Belgian endive (from Europe); watercress (from Florida); and the chicories (from Florida, California, and Arizona).

Remember that oranges, lemons, grapefruit, and avocados are all at their cheapest now.

**12 ounces–1 pound green leaves
(e.g., chicory, Belgian endive,
watercress, Chinese cabbage,
spinach leaves, lettuce)**
**1 tablespoon wine or cider vinegar
(or juice of ½ lemon)**
**3–4 tablespoons olive oil or other
vegetable oil**
**salt and freshly ground black
pepper to taste**
½ clove garlic, crushed (optional)

*Nowadays, there are many leafy green alternatives to the tissue-
paper-thin, hot-house lettuce that is so ubiquitous in the winter months.
Buy the crispiest lettuce you can find and mix it with the sharper
tasting Belgian endive, bitter chicory, shredded Chinese cabbage,
peppery watercress, or young spinach leaves. Also look out for the
mild escarole, red radicchio, and lamb's lettuce or corn salad. Buy
small quantities of several types of greens (they all keep exceptionally
well, if wrapped, in the bottom of the refrigerator) and mix the
textures, tones, leaf shapes, and flavors.*

Wash the leaves and drain them well (the inner leaves of some
of the close-hearted varieties do not need washing), handling the leaves
with care. Tear the larger leaves into small pieces and put them in
a mixing bowl. Make the dressing by combining the remaining
ingredients, and pour it over the salad just before serving. Gently
toss the salad and serve.

VARIATION

Walnut oil is expensive but excellent with green salad. Make the
salad and dribble a little walnut oil over it. Add even less wine or
cider vinegar, toss well but gently, and serve.

Winter Salad Bowl

4 ounces small florets of
   cauliflower
4 ounces green beans, topped,
   tailed, and cut diagonally into
   2-inch lengths
4 ounces carrots, peeled, cut in
   half and then into sticks
4 ounces fresh or frozen peas
4 ounces cooked beets, sliced
1 small head of lettuce, shredded
1 tablespoon lemon juice
3 tablespoons olive oil (or other
   vegetable oil)
salt and black pepper to taste

A colorful and nutritious salad of lightly cooked winter vege-tables. The vegetables given are only suggestions, and you could use other combinations that suit your taste, according to availability.

Bring a small pan of salted water to a boil and separately parboil the cauliflower, green beans, carrots, and peas for 5–10 minutes or until each is just *al dente* or firm to the bite. (The process can be sped up by using more than one pan of boiling water.) Drain the vegetables and allow them to cool.

Place the shredded lettuce in a serving bowl and put the cauli-flower in the center of the bed of lettuce. Arrange the green beans, carrots, peas, and beets around the cauliflower in separate groups.

Combine the lemon juice, oil, salt, and black pepper and mix well. Carefully dribble a little of this dressing over each of the clumps of vegetables, reserving about 1 tablespoon of the dressing. Chill the salad for 30 minutes, and then sprinkle the remaining dressing over all.

Spinach and Apple Salad with Lime Dressing

1 pound fresh spinach, washed
   and drained
2 medium-sized eating apples,
   chilled, cored, quartered, and
   chopped into small pieces
2 tablespoons vegetable oil
1 tablespoon lime juice
salt and black pepper to taste

In the autumn and winter limes are sometimes as cheap as lemons, and lime juice is a delicious alternative to lemon juice in a salad dressing. In this salad, the sharpness of the lime juice sets off the sweetness of the apple, and the flavor also enhances the sometimes harsh taste of spinach.

Remove any thick spinach stalks; finely shred the leaves. Combine the oil and lime juice and whisk well together. Mix the spinach and the chilled apples, pour the dressing over this mixture, add salt and black pepper, and toss well.

half a red cabbage
4 tablespoons walnut or olive oil
3 tablespoons lemon juice
2 large oranges
1 large eating apple
2 ounces walnut halves
1 banana

A sweet and sour salad, crunchy and colorful, good with hearty lamb stews. Also ideal as a winter lunch with a wedge of tangy Cheddar or Colby cheese.

Shred the cabbage finely and toss with the oil and lemon juice. Leave to marinate in the refrigerator for 1 hour. Peel the oranges and separate them into segments. Core and chop the apple into large segments. Peel and slice the banana into thick rings. Add the fruit and walnuts to the cabbage. Toss all the ingredients lightly and serve.

12 ounces white cabbage, finely
    shredded
4 ounces red cabbage, finely
    shredded
2 teaspoons lemon juice
1 medium-sized eating apple,
    cored and cut into thin
    matchsticks
2 tablespoons milk
2 medium egg yolks
1 teaspoon prepared English
    mustard
1 teaspoon honey
1 tablespoon vegetable oil
4 tablespoons wine vinegar
salt and black pepper to taste
2 tablespoons sour cream

This is an unusual way of serving coleslaw but it's rather nice on a cold winter's day, served as a side salad to a main dish or with hot soup and bread as a light meal. The coleslaw can also be heated through and served very hot as a vegetable dish.

Combine the white and red cabbage in a serving bowl. Stir the lemon juice into the apple and then add it to the cabbage.

Make the dressing. Combine the milk, egg yolks, mustard, honey, oil, vinegar, and seasoning in a blender or mixing bowl and beat smooth. Transfer the mixture to the top of a double boiler or to a small heavy pan over a very low heat. Stirring all the time, cook the mixture until it starts to thicken. Put a little of it into a bowl and stir in the sour cream. Pour this back into the pan and heat, stirring constantly, until it is very hot.

Pour the dressing over the cabbage, mix well, grind some black pepper over the top, and serve at once.

Two-Color Cabbage and Tangerine Salad

SERVES 4 TO 6

4 ounces finely shredded
   white cabbage
4 ounces finely shredded
   red cabbage
2–3 tangerines, peeled and sliced
2 tablespoons olive or sesame oil
1 tablespoon lemon juice
½ teaspoon salt
6 radishes, trimmed, chopped

Colorful, tasty, and with contrasting textures, the tangerines give this salad a Christmas look.

Combine the shredded cabbage and tangerine slices and mix well together. In a small bowl stir together the oil, lemon juice, and salt and pour over the salad.

Toss the salad gently and then garnish it with the chopped radishes. Serve at once or cover and refrigerate until needed.

Fennel, Leek, and Tomato Salad

1 medium-sized fennel bulb,
   trimmed and finely sliced
2 medium-sized leeks, trimmed
   and very finely sliced
12 ounces tomatoes, sliced
4 tablespoons olive oil
1 tablespoon lemon juice
salt and black pepper

Leeks make a pleasant change from onions in a winter salad. From midautumn onward, we find that tomatoes grown in hot climates under natural conditions have much more flavor than those grown in artificial or semi-artificial conditions. This salad needs good tomatoes and good olive oil.

Place the fennel, leeks, and tomatoes in a mixing bowl. Dress them with the olive oil and the lemon juice, and season with the salt and pepper. Toss the vegetables gently but thoroughly together so that they are well-coated in the dressing.

Broccoli with Hot Coconut Sauce

2 tablespoons sesame oil or other
  vegetable oil
1 medium onion, chopped
2 cloves garlic, crushed
3 ounces freshly grated coconut
  or 5 ounces flaked coconut
juice of 1 lemon
pinch cayenne pepper
salt to taste
water or milk
1½ pounds broccoli or other
  vegetables

This salad dish, like Gado-Gado (page 123), is Southeast Asian in origin. For it to be truly authentic, freshly grated coconut should be used, but dried coconut is fine. (If you use fresh coconut in this salad, remember that coconuts are very perishable and should be kept in the refrigerator and used as soon as possible.)

Green beans, carrots, peppers or eggplant, or mixed cooked vegetables may also be used in this recipe, so long as the coconut sauce is prepared in the same way. Serve as a side salad to a curry or other spicy meal, or as an unusual starter.

Heat the oil in a frying pan and add the onion and garlic. Stir-fry until the onion is softened. Add the coconut and continue stir-frying until the coconut is just lightly browned. Transfer the contents of the pan to a blender or food processor, add the lemon juice, cayenne pepper, and salt to taste. Switch the machine on and add enough water or milk to form a thickish sauce that will just run easily off a spoon. Pour the sauce into a small pan and heat through gently, stirring; keep hot.

Cut any tough stem ends off the broccoli and divide it into florets. Cook the broccoli for 6–8 minutes in enough boiling, salted water just to cover. Drain and rinse under cold running water until cold. Pour the hot sauce over the broccoli and serve.

Chinese Greens with Peanut Dressing

8 ounces Chinese greens
  (*choi-sum*), washed, trimmed
  if necessary, and tied into
  bundles
salt
2 tablespoons creamy peanut
  butter
1 tablespoon tamari (natural
  soy sauce)

This salad is very good with Chinese flowering cabbage (choi-sum). This green leafy vegetable with a mild flavor is most popular with the Chinese. It is available at most Chinese grocery stores all year round. If choi-sum *is unavailable, the same dressing is good with Chinese chard (bok choy).*

Drop the bundles of greens into a pan of lightly salted, slowly boiling water for 2 minutes. Drain the greens, separate them from the bundles and immediately rinse them under cold water until cooled.

Chop the greens into 1-inch lengths. Mix together the peanut butter and soy sauce (add a little oil if the mixture is too thick). Toss the greens in this dressing and serve them in individual deep serving bowls.

Parsnip and Date Salad

3 large parsnips, peeled and grated
8 fresh dates or dried dates (pour
  boiling water over them and
  drain), chopped
1 teaspoon fresh rosemary,
  chopped
Vinaigrette Dressing (page 125)
  to taste

Parsnips have a distinctive, sweet flavor that harmonizes well with dates, their unlikely companion in this salad. Use fresh dates if they are available; otherwise use dried dates. Rosemary is not used often in salads, but here its slightly bitter flavor offsets the sweetness of the fruit and vegetables.

Combine the parsnips, dates, and rosemary, add the dressing to taste, toss well, and serve.

½ small crisp lettuce (iceberg or
  Romaine), washed
2 medium carrots, peeled and
  finely grated
2 medium oranges, peeled, pith
  removed, separated into
  segments
4 ounces dates (fresh or dessert),
  pitted and chopped
1 ounce chopped freshly
  toasted almonds
2 tablespoons lemon juice
1 teaspoon extra fine granulated
  sugar
¼ teaspoon salt
1 tablespoon orange flower water
  (optional)

This exotic salad is inspired by a similar Moroccan salad. It is good as an appetizer, as a side salad for serving with a hot, spicy main dish, or as the final course of a meal.

Separate the lettuce leaves and prepare a bed of them in a glass serving bowl. Place the grated carrot in the middle of the lettuce leaves and arrange the orange segments around it. Put the chopped dates on top of the carrot and sprinkle the toasted almonds over all.

Combine the lemon juice, sugar, salt, and orange flower water and sprinkle the mixture over the salad. Chill and serve.

Winter Fig and Walnut Salad

SERVES 6

8 ounces white cabbage, finely
    shredded
4 medium carrots, peeled and
    grated
1 small onion, finely chopped
1 medium-sized cooking apple,
    cored and grated
4 ounces dried figs, sliced
4 ounces walnut halves
Tofu Dressing (page 132)
1 dessert apple, cored and thinly
    sliced
juice of ½ orange

A colorful, crunchy salad with a tasty and nutritious tofu (bean curd) dressing. The recipe is adapted from a recipe in David Scott and Clair Golding's book, The True Vegetarian Cookery Book.

Combine the cabbage, carrots, onion, cooking apple, figs (reserve a few for garnishing), and walnuts (reserve a few for garnishing) in a mixing bowl. Add the dressing and toss the mixture in it.

Transfer the salad to a serving bowl and arrange the apple slices over the top. Sprinkle the orange juice on top, garnish with the reserved figs and walnuts, and serve at once.

Spinach, Mushroom, and Croûton Salad

8 ounces summer spinach
8 ounces small mushrooms
24 croûtons (page 131)
salt and black pepper to taste
juice of ½ lemon
6 tablespoons olive oil
2 tablespoons white wine vinegar

A first course salad of dark green spinach leaves and crunchy white mushrooms and croûtons.

Wash the spinach and drain it well. Tear the leaves into large pieces, discarding the stalks. Place the spinach in a bowl. Wipe and slice the mushrooms and squeeze the lemon juice over them.

Put salt and pepper into a small bowl, add the olive oil and wine vinegar, and whisk until blended. Scatter the mushrooms and croûtons over the spinach, pour the dressing over, toss thoroughly, and serve.

Navy Beans in Rich Tomato Sauce

6 ounces dried navy beans,
    soaked overnight and drained
8 fluid ounces Basic Tomato Sauce
    (page 129)
½ bunch spring onions, washed,
    trimmed of coarse green leaves
    and finely sliced
1 clove garlic, well crushed
1 teaspoon dried oregano
1 tablespoon chopped parsley
a few fresh thyme leaves
salt and black pepper to taste

This is vastly superior to anything you can get in cans, and if you really want to, you can eat it hot on toast.

Cook the beans in fresh unsalted water until tender (about 1–1½ hours). Drain the beans and combine them with the tomato sauce, onions, and garlic. Add the herbs and the seasonings and set aside to cool. Adjust the seasoning when the salad is cold.

Red Cabbage in Juniper Cream and Yogurt Sauce

SERVES 6

1 pound red cabbage
3 fluid ounces natural yogurt
3 fluid ounces whipping cream
12 juniper berries, ground or
    finely crushed
2 teaspoons cider or wine vinegar
salt to taste

A colorful salad that goes particularly well with cold meats.

Remove any discolored outer leaves and the bitter core from the cabbage. Now shred it finely (if you are using a knife, use a stainless steel one). Combine the cabbage with the other ingredients, mix them well together, and serve.

16 fluid ounces natural yogurt, chilled
salt and black pepper to taste
4 soft-boiled eggs, shelled and quartered
½ teaspoon dried mint
2 tablespoons olive oil
½ teaspoon cumin seeds, finely ground
½ teaspoon coriander seeds, finely ground
1 heaped teaspoon paprika

This unusual appetizer initially looks plain, but it is transformed before serving by the last-minute addition of hot, aromatic olive oil, which pours lava-like over the surface of the yogurt.

Season the yogurt to taste with salt and black pepper, and divide it among four small plates. Top each plate with the quartered eggs arranged in rosette fashion. Keep these prepared plates chilled until serving time.

Put the olive oil in a small saucepan, add the cumin and coriander, and bring the pan to a medium heat. Remove from heat and stir in the paprika. Pour some of the hot oil mixture over each egg and yogurt salad and serve immediately.

VARIATION

Replace the soft-boiled eggs with poached or fried eggs. This is a good method but slightly more troublesome than that given in the recipe.

Indonesian Rice Salad

2 fluid ounces orange juice

2 tablespoons sesame seed or other vegetable oil

2 tablespoons tamari

salt and pepper to taste

8 ounces long-grain brown or white rice, cooked and cooled to room temperature

2 ounces bean sprouts, washed

1 medium green pepper, core and seeds removed and chopped

1 stick celery, chopped

2 spring onions, chopped

2 ounces roasted almonds or cashews

2 ounces sultana raisins, plumped up with a little boiling water and then drained

4 ounces fresh or canned pineapple chunks

This sounds an unlikely choice for a winter salad, but all the ingredients are easily available and it brings a hint of sunny tropics to a gloomy winter's day.

Make the dressing. Combine the first 3 ingredients and season to taste. Mix together all the remaining ingredients. Pour the dressing over the salad. Toss well together and chill slightly before serving.

VARIATIONS

• Serve the salad on a bed of greens.
• Add thinly sliced water chestnuts or bamboo shoots.
• Garnish the salad with a little dry-roasted flaked coconut.

Spiced Beet and Walnut Salad

1 pound beets, cooked and peeled
1 medium onion, finely chopped
4 ounces walnuts, crushed
2 cloves garlic, crushed
2 tablespoons parsley, chopped,
   plus extra for garnish
2 tablespoons wine vinegar
1 teaspoon ground coriander
salt and cayenne pepper to taste
1 teaspoon dried dill weed
   (optional)

Not many years ago, Paddy used to drive regularly from Edinburgh to Liverpool on a Sunday night. With the journey over three-quarters done, it was his practice to stop at a Lancashire pub for one of their homemade hot-pot pies and a pint of Thwaite's best bitter. It was just a penny extra for a rough beet and onion salad that always tasted unbelievably good. Hunger and nostalgia must be two of the best triggers of gastric juices. Here is a delicious beet salad that requires neither for its enjoyment.

Cut the beets into fine slices or large julienne strips. Place these in a mixing bowl and combine with the rest of the ingredients. Mix very thoroughly and check the seasoning before turning the salad into a serving bowl. Garnish with the reserved parsley.

White Bean and Sweet-Sour Beet Salad

2 medium-sized cooked beets,
   diced
1 tablespoon butter
2 teaspoons cider vinegar
2 teaspoons honey
8 ounces cooked white beans
salt to taste
2 tablespoons sour cream
   (or plain yogurt)

Any type of cooked bean may be used to make this salad but white beans contrast well with the red beets. This is a filling and tasty winter salad good with a main meal, but also fine as a light lunch with bread and cheese.

Put the beets in a pan with the butter and gently heat through. Stir in the vinegar and honey. Continue heating to melt the honey and coat the beets in the sauce.

Pour this mixture over the beans, stirring well; salt to taste and set aside in refrigerator to chill. Serve dressed in sour cream (or yogurt).

SERVES 8

8 ounces white radish (daikon) about 8 inches long
2 medium-sized carrots
1 teaspoon salt
3 fluid ounces rice or cider vinegar
1 teaspoon tamari (natural soy sauce)
1 tablespoon white sugar

Daikon, one of the ingredients in this salad, is the traditional Japanese variety of radish. It is pure white and grows to about 12 inches in length. Mild in flavor, it is used both fresh (usually grated) as a salad vegetable or garnish, and pickled. Daikon is now grown here and is becoming generally available, especially in Chinese grocery stores.

This is a versatile salad that can be served as an appetizer or as a side dish with the main course, or on its own with drinks and salted nuts. The salad can be served within one hour of its preparation, but it is not at its best until at least one day later. It keeps well (up to 2 weeks in an airtight container in the refrigerator), so it's worth making more than you immediately need.

Peel the white radish and scrape the carrots; cut them both into matchsticks about 1½ inches in length. Put them into a large mixing bowl and sprinkle with the salt. Leave for 30 minutes and then gather the radish/carrot mixture in both hands and gently squeeze out all the water you can.

Combine the vinegar, tamari, and sugar and add the mixture to the vegetables. Cover and refrigerate. Serve, if you wish, after one hour, but the salad is at its best if eaten about 8 hours later.

Marinated Eggplant Salad

SERVES 4 TO 6

2 small eggplants, sliced
3 fluid ounces olive oil
2 fluid ounces wine vinegar
2 cloves garlic, crushed
1 tablespoon lemon juice
1 teaspoon dried basil
salt and black pepper to taste
½ cucumber, thinly sliced
2 medium tomatoes, quartered
2 tablespoons natural yogurt

Here cooked eggplant slices are marinated for 2 hours in an oil and vinegar dressing and then tossed with tomatoes and cucumber and garnished with yogurt. This is a salad that needs some advance planning. It has a Middle Eastern flavor and is good served with pita bread as an hors d'oeuvre or as an accompaniment to mildly spiced rice dishes.

Lightly brush the eggplant slices on both sides with some of the oil and broil them until just browned and tender enough to push a fork through easily. Cut the eggplant slices into quarters.

Combine the remaining oil, vinegar, garlic, lemon juice, basil, salt, and black pepper to taste in a bowl and mix well. Add the eggplant while it is still warm. Transfer the bowl to a refrigerator and leave for about 2 hours. Stir in the cucumber and tomatoes, top with a dollop of yogurt, and serve.

Pasta with Green Garlic Dressing

2 cloves garlic, skinned
5 fluid ounces Green Vinaigrette
    Dressing (page 125)
½–1 fresh jalapeño chili pepper
    (preferably red)
1¼ pounds cooked, cold, lightly
    oiled pasta
salt and pepper to taste
thick cream and lightly chopped
    parsley to garnish

A simple and substantial salad, which is also an excellent way of using leftover spaghetti—though it is worth making at any time with pasta of all shapes. Green Garlic Dressing is also excellent with lightly cooked cauliflower.

Blend the garlic thoroughly with the Green Vinaigrette Dressing. Add the fresh chili and blend until it has broken down into small, but still visible, flecks. Pour the dressing onto the pasta in a mixing bowl and toss well. Taste for pepper and salt.

Divide into individual portions and top each with a dollop of thick cream or Strained Yogurt (page 128) and a sprinkling of lightly chopped parsley.

Spiced Yogurt and Onion Salad

10 fluid ounces natural yogurt
1 tablespoon neutral vegetable oil
(such as sunflower or peanut)
1 teaspoon black mustard seeds
good pinch Madras curry powder
salt to taste
2 medium-sized onions, finely
sliced

A very simple, refreshing salad from Sri Lanka, this makes an excellent accompaniment to all those robust winter dishes such as lamb or beef stew, shepherd's pie, or cheese and potato au gratin.

Spoon the yogurt into a mixing bowl. Pour the oil into a small pan over medium heat. Add the mustard seeds to the oil and watch closely. Remove the pan from the heat as soon as the seeds start popping and spluttering. Add the seeds to the yogurt, together with the curry powder and the salt, and beat well. Stir in the finely sliced onions, check the seasoning, and serve at once.

Sushi Rice Salad

SERVES 4 TO 6

12 ounces white short-grained rice
2¼ cups water
4 tablespoons rice or cider vinegar
3 tablespoons white sugar
½ teaspoon salt
3 tablespoons vegetable oil
1 egg, beaten
1 tablespoon tamari (natural soy
sauce)
1 medium carrot, peeled, sliced
into thin rounds
1 medium onion, finely diced
1 stick celery, finely chopped
2 ounces mushrooms, quartered
2 teaspoons finely sliced pickled
ginger for garnish (optional)

Sushi is a general word used to describe a variety of Japanese dishes in which the basic ingredient is cooked rice seasoned with vinegar and sugar. In the most popular type of sushi the rice is formed into different shapes which are then topped with a selection of garnishes (called nigiri-sushi). *Here we make* chira-sushi *or, as it is in translation, vinegared rice mingled with vegetables. This is a substantial salad, and it makes a good main course or buffet meal.*

First wash the rice. Wash it well by stirring it vigorously in a bowl or pan in lots of water. Let the grains settle and carefully pour off the milky residue. Repeat the process until the water remains almost clear (this will be a quick process with good quality rice; it will take longer with loosely packed rice).

Drain the rice and place it in a heavy pan. Add the water, cover, and bring to the boil quickly. Turn the heat down and allow it to simmer for 15 minutes. Turn off the heat and allow the rice to stand for 5–10 minutes. Turn the rice into a non-metallic mixing bowl and set aside.

Combine the vinegar, sugar, and salt and bring the mixture to a boil, stirring. Pour this dressing over the hot rice. Turn the rice gently with a wet wooden spoon in one hand while with the other hand fan the rice with a flat pan lid or rolled-up newspaper. This cools the rice quickly and gives it an authentic shine. Set the rice aside.

Brush a large frying pan with a little of the oil. Beat the egg with 1 teaspoon of the tamari and prepare a thin omelette in the frying pan. Remove the omelette and cut it into thin strips. Set them aside.

In the same pan heat two-thirds of the remaining oil and sauté the carrot, onion, and celery for 2−3 minutes. Set them aside. Heat the remaining oil in the pan and sauté the mushrooms for a few minutes until just cooked. Remove them from the heat and stir in the remaining tamari.

Gently mix the sushi rice with the cooked vegetables and mushrooms in sauce. Transfer the mixture to a serving dish and mold it into a mound. Garnish the top with strips of omelette and pickled ginger. Serve chilled or at room temperature.

Stuffed Apple Salad

4 red dessert apples, cored and quartered
2 stalks celery, finely chopped
2 ounces unsalted peanuts
2 ounces whole hazelnuts
2 ounces sultana raisins
4 fluid ounces natural yogurt (or mayonnaise)
1 teaspoon lemon juice
1 tablespoon finely chopped parsley

This is a variation on a Waldorf salad in which the standard ingredients (except the apple) are combined and then used to stuff small dessert apples. The individual salads look their best if served in small fruit bowls, so that the quartered apples are held in a rosette shape with the celery and nut stuffing resting in the middle.

Arrange the apples in individual bowls so that the sides are supported and the apple forms a rosette. Combine the remaining ingredients, except the parsley, and mix well.

Divide the mixture among the four apples and spoon it into the center of each. Garnish with chopped parsley and serve at once.

Three-Bean Salad

SERVES 4 TO 6

**4 ounces red kidney beans
(soaked overnight)
4 ounces white beans (soaked
overnight)
4 ounces chick-peas (soaked
overnight)
4 parsley stalks + 2 tablespoons
finely chopped parsley
1 bay leaf
2 sprigs of fresh thyme or
1 teaspoon dried thyme
½ medium onion, finely chopped
1 clove garlic, crushed
1 tablespoon wine or cider vinegar
2 tablespoons olive oil (or other
vegetable oil)
½ teaspoon cumin seeds, ground
salt and black pepper to taste**

This robust salad will keep you well fueled on a winter's day. The cooked beans are mixed with lots of fresh parsley and this makes all the difference to the flavor of the finished salad. The salad goes well with salami, crumbly tangy cheese, hard-boiled eggs, and pickled fish.

Drain the beans and rinse them. Put them in a saucepan and cover with unsalted water. Bring beans rapidly to a boil, boil hard for 10 minutes, and then reduce to a simmer. Add the parsley stalks, bay leaf, and thyme. Cover and cook until all the beans are tender (about 1–1½ hours).

Drain the beans (reserving the liquid for later use as stock) and discard the spent herbs. Put the hot beans in a mixing bowl and add the remaining ingredients. Mix well and leave to cool. Adjust seasoning, if necessary, before serving.

VARIATION

Use leftover cooked beans or separately cooked beans to make the salad. Canned beans can also be used for convenience. In this case use only canned chick-peas and canned red kidney beans.

Hot Chick-Pea Salad

9 ounces chick-peas, washed
  and soaked overnight
1 small onion or shallot
1 small carrot
1 bay leaf and a sprig of thyme
2 cloves garlic
4½ fluid ounces olive oil
1 tablespoon salt
2 red chilies, diced
vinegar (optional)
chopped onion (optional)

Paddy was once served a very basic version of this salad from a vast cooking pot in a Moroccan street market. A steaming ladle of chick-peas, a pointed finger, and a nod in the direction of a thick potage of crushed garlic and olive oil, another nod in the direction of a bowl containing a mixture of ground dried red chilies and salt. An earthy, powerful, and tasty dish, the essence of which is the rich vapor of olive oil rising from the hot chick-peas.

Drain the chick-peas and put them and the rest of the ingredients into a saucepan. Cover these ingredients with unsalted water or, if possible, the liquid residue from cooked spinach. Bring the contents of the saucepan to a boil, cover, and simmer slowly for 1½ hours or until the chick-peas are tender.

Arrange on the table one small bowl containing the cloves of garlic, crushed and steeped in the olive oil, and another bowl containing the salt ground together with the diced red chilies. Some people may also want vinegar and some chopped onion at hand. Spoon the hot drained chick-peas into four small bowls and let each person choose his or her own flavorings.

Russian Winter Salad

SERVES 6

6 ounces cooked beets, peeled
   and diced
6 ounces cooked but firm
   potatoes, peeled and diced
2 medium-sized eating apples,
   cored and diced
2 medium-sized carrots, peeled
   and diced
1 tablespoon prepared mustard
4 tablespoons vegetable oil
4 tablespoons sour cream
salt to taste

A substantial, mustard-hot salad dressed in sour cream and designed to keep the Siberian cold at bay.

Combine the beets, potatoes, apples, and carrots. Stir the mustard into the oil to form a paste. Stir this into the beet mixture and set it aside for 1 hour. Just before serving, stir in the sour cream.

Four-Root Salad

1 celeriac root (about 10 ounces)
3 medium carrots
1 medium parsnip
2 medium-sized, parcooked beets
2 tablespoons chopped parsley
Vinaigrette Dressing (page 125)

Enjoy this salad at its best in early winter when the newly lifted roots are at their sweetest and most tender. Be careful to prepare the celeriac as indicated on page 15. Mustard-flavored vinaigrette also goes well with this salad.

Peel and coarsely grate, chop, or cut into julienne strips all the root vegetables. Combine the celeriac, carrots, parsnip, and parsley and mix well, then gently fold in the beets. Turn the vegetables onto a presentation dish and dress liberally with a well-seasoned vinaigrette dressing.

SERVES 4 TO 6

2 tablespoons sesame oil
3 tablespoons tamari (natural soy
sauce)
3 tablespoons cider vinegar
1 tablespoon water
1 teaspoon clear honey
1 clove garlic, crushed
2 blocks 12-ounce tofu (bean
curd), cut into 1-inch cubes
2 stalks celery, finely chopped
2 ounces mushrooms, washed
and sliced
4 ounces Chinese or white
cabbage, finely shredded

Tofu or bean curd is a soybean product. It is soft and white with a custard-like texture which easily absorbs the flavors of other ingredients. Tofu is now readily available in Chinese food stores, supermarkets, and health-food shops. It is sold in small blocks or cakes and is stored loose in cold water (or in vacuum-sealed packs). It will keep in a container of water for 3–4 days in the refrigerator. Tofu is a rich source of protein, vitamins, and minerals.

Combine the oil, tamari, vinegar, water, honey, and garlic and mix well together. Put two-thirds of this mixture into a large shallow bowl or container and add the tofu cubes. Leave them to marinate in the refrigerator for 1 hour.

Transfer the tofu and marinade to a serving bowl and gently stir in the celery, mushrooms, and cabbage. Add the remaining dressing, carefully toss the salad, and serve.

2 tablespoons wine vinegar
2 tablespoons clear honey
2 tablespoons tamari or other
  soy sauce
2 tablespoons peanut or other
  vegetable oil
2 cloves garlic, crushed
1 medium onion, finely chopped
2 medium-sized red or green
  peppers, seeded and cut into
  strips
12 ounces white cabbage, finely
  shredded
½ bunch radishes, trimmed and
  sliced
6 ounces bean sprouts

The vegetables in this salad are very lightly cooked, mixed with a sweet and sour dressing, and then allowed to cool before serving. Don't overcook the vegetables or the finished salad will have no crunch.

Combine the vinegar, honey, and soy sauce. Heat the oil in a frying pan or wok and stir-fry the garlic and onion for 1 minute. Add the pepper and cabbage and stir-fry for another 5 minutes. Add the radishes and bean sprouts and cook for 1 minute.

Stir the vinegar mixture into the vegetables. Transfer them to a serving bowl and allow to cool before serving.

Potato and Beet with Horseradish Cream

1½ pounds potatoes, boiled in
   their skins and left to cool
4 fluid ounces Horseradish Sauce
   (page 133) or any name brand
3 fluid ounces whipping cream
1 medium-sized beet, uncooked,
   but peeled
salt to taste
cream to garnish

Potatoes are bland and they need assertive companions to put a bit of life into them. The more mature potatoes are, the greater their need for this kind of company. At different times of the year we will have added mint, yogurt, spinach, lemon juice, sorrel, vinegar, sweet peppers, ginger, and chili peppers, and now, in winter, we use horseradish.

Peel the potatoes, cut them into small bite-sized pieces, and place them in a mixing bowl. Coarsely grate ¾ of the beet and arrange over the potatoes. Spoon the horseradish sauce and the whipping cream over the vegetables, season with salt, and mix well.

Turn the salad onto a serving plate, top with a dab of cream, and grate the remaining beet over the salad.

Sweet Corn and Kidney Bean Salad

A good, colorful standby for winter, tasty and simple enough to produce at any season.

4 ounces dried red kidney beans,
   soaked overnight
1 medium can sweet corn
   (8 ounces), drained
1 small onion, spring onion, or
   shallot, sliced
salt
4 fluid ounces Speedy Chili
   Dressing (page 130)

Drain the beans, cover them with fresh water, bring to a boil, and boil hard for 10 minutes. Cover, reduce to a simmer, and cook until the beans are tender (about 1 – 1½ hours). Drain and allow to cool.

Stir the beans, sweet corn, and onion together in a salad bowl, lightly season with salt, and then stir in the dressing. Serve at once.

Brown Rice and Bean Salad

SERVES 4 TO 6

4 ounces dried red kidney beans
(or chick-peas or white beans),
soaked overnight, then cooked
and drained

5 ounces brown rice, cooked,
rinsed, and cooled

3 tablespoons Mayonnaise
(page 126)

3 tablespoons cider vinegar

2 cloves garlic, crushed

1 tablespoon lemon juice

2 tablespoons finely chopped
parsley

salt and black pepper to taste

1 medium carrot, peeled and
cut into matchsticks

1 green pepper, seeded and diced

1 stick celery, finely chopped

Rice and beans are complementary protein partners, and, weight for weight, this salad has the same amount of usable protein as a piece of steak. Do not, however, think it will be heavy and boring. The finished salad looks moist, colorful, and tempting, and most important, it tastes good.

Combine the beans, rice, mayonnaise, vinegar, garlic, lemon juice, parsley, salt, and black pepper and gently mix well together. Set the mixture aside in the refrigerator to chill for 30 minutes and to give the beans and rice time to absorb the dressing.

Toss in the carrot, pepper, and celery and serve.

6 ounces dried white beans,
   soaked overnight
6 ounces small elbow or shell
   pasta
1 tablespoon olive oil
1 clove garlic, crushed
1 teaspoon prepared mustard
4 tablespoons Vinaigrette
   Dressing (page 125)
2 tablespoons chopped parsley
   (preferably the flat Italian
   variety)
2 tablespoons ground, roasted
   cumin seeds
salt and black pepper to taste

Another excellent hearty winter salad with that protein-rich combination of legumes and grains. Here this combination also provides an interesting contrast in textures.

Cook the beans in unsalted water until tender (about 1–1½ hours), drain, and set aside to cool. Cook the pasta in salted water until it is *al dente* or just firm to the bite; pour into a colander to drain. Gently toss the pasta to shake any water out of its cavities.

Combine the beans, pasta, and olive oil in a small bowl and mix well. Stir in the remaining ingredients and check the seasoning. Serve at room temperature.

8 ounces large green or brown
   lentils, well picked over,
   washed, and soaked for 2 hours
1 medium-sized onion, finely
   chopped
4 tablespoons olive oil
½ teaspoon ground cumin seeds
salt and black pepper to taste
5 ounces long-grain rice

FOR THE GARNISH

1 medium-sized onion, sliced
   vertically into crescent-shaped
   slices
4 tablespoons vegetable oil
5 fluid ounces natural yogurt
salt and black pepper to taste

This dish is popular in the Arab world. It is exceptionally nutritious, and like so many peasant dishes, very satisfying. Accompany this dish with a light green salad and a plate of dressed, sliced tomatoes.

Drain the lentils, cover them with fresh water, and bring them to a boil. Reduce the heat and simmer the lentils for 20 minutes or until they are barely tender. Meanwhile, gently fry the chopped onion in the oil until it is soft and golden. Add the cooked onion and the seasonings to the lentils and cook briefly before adding the rice. Add water to cover and bring back to the boil. Reduce the heat, cover the pan, and simmer for 20 minutes or until the rice is cooked. Check during the period that there is enough water in the pan to prevent the rice from drying out. Check the seasoning and stir the food before spooning it onto a serving dish and leaving it to cool.

Make the garnish. Fry the onion slices in very hot oil until they are dark brown and beginning to crisp. Remove and drain on paper towels. Beat the seasonings and the yogurt together and pour this sauce into a depression made in the mound of rice and lentils. Lay the fried onions over the surface of the yogurt.

Gado-Gado

SERVES 4 TO 6

FOR THE SPICY PEANUT SAUCE

1 tablespoon vegetable oil
1 clove garlic, crushed
½ medium onion, finely diced
½ dried red chili, seeds removed, chopped, or ¼ teaspoon hot pepper sauce
4 ounces peanut butter
2 teaspoons brown sugar
2 teaspoons lemon juice
8 fluid ounces water (or the same volume fresh or canned coconut milk, if available)
salt to taste

VEGETABLES

2 medium potatoes, peeled and cut into even-sized chunks
4 ounces green beans, topped, tailed, and strung, cut into 2-inch lengths
2 medium carrots, peeled, cut in half and then thickly sliced lengthwise
½ medium cucumber, sliced
4 ounces bean sprouts, washed, drained
½ head crisp lettuce, washed, chopped
1 hard-boiled egg, peeled and sliced for garnish

Gado-Gado is a popular Indonesian salad dish consisting of a mixture of raw and cold cooked vegetables arranged on a serving dish. It is served with a spicy peanut sauce that is either poured over the vegetables or served in a side bowl. It is light, crunchy, tasty, and good for you. The vegetables suggested in the ingredients list may be changed to suit availability or personal preference. If you do not like moderately hot food, use less chili pepper than suggested (or omit it altogether) in the peanut sauce.

Heat the oil in a small pan and sauté the garlic, onion, and chili pepper until softened. Put the contents of the pan into a blender or food processor and add the peanut butter, sugar, lemon juice, and water or coconut milk. Process until smooth and then pour the mixture back into the pan. Bring the mixture to a gentle boil, stirring occasionally; season to taste with salt and allow to simmer slowly.

Cook the potatoes until just tender, and then drain and rinse them under cold running water until cold. Boil the beans and carrots in salted water to cover for 5 minutes only. Drain and rinse them under cold running water until cold.

Arrange the cucumber, bean sprouts, lettuce, cooked potatoes, and parcooked beans and carrots on a serving dish, garnish with slices of hard-boiled egg, and serve with the hot peanut sauce poured over, or in a separate bowl.

Dressings

Included here are all the dressings called for in the recipes in the main part of the book. There are all types—from a basic oil and vinegar dressing to creamier dressings made with tahini, yogurt, tofu, and avocado, to chili and horseradish dressings, and good, old-fashioned mayonnaise.

Starchy salads, particularly those containing beans, benefit from being dressed while they are still warm—this enables the flavorings to penetrate more deeply. Taste and add more dressing, if necessary, when the salads are cold.

Dressings are often the most expensive part of a salad and to add too much is a waste of money. Do make sure, however, that you mix in the dressing well, or the amounts we have given may not seem enough.

Vinaigrette Dressing

MAKES 5 FLUID OUNCES

4½ fluid ounces vegetable oil
2 tablespoons wine vinegar, cider
   vinegar, or lemon juice
salt and pepper to taste
1 teaspoon prepared mustard
   (optional)

Vary your vinaigrette dressings according to the ingredients with which they are to be served. We find that heavy, dried bean or starchy root vegetable salads may be best with a vinaigrette dressing with a ratio of 3 parts oil to 1 part vinegar, while strongly flavored greens are best with a 4 to 1 oil/vinegar ratio, and sweet, delicate lettuce is best with a 5 to 1 ratio.

We prefer to use a light olive oil. Since its flavor would be wasted if you were going to add strong spices to the dressing, in that case use peanut or sunflower oil instead. Mustard is the most usual addition to the basic vinaigrette. It serves a two-fold purpose; first, to give "bite" when used with rich or slightly sweet foods like avocados or root vegetables, and second, it helps to emulsify the oil and vinegar so that the dressing clings to the salad instead of running off. If you are going to use chopped fresh herbs in the vinaigrette, add them just before you dress the salad.

Place all ingredients in a bowl or blender and beat or blend well. Test and adjust seasoning if necessary.

Green Vinaigrette Dressing

MAKES 5 FLUID OUNCES

4½ fluid ounces olive oil
2 tablespoons lemon juice
2 ounces (½ a large bunch)
   parsley, larger stems removed
1 teaspoon prepared mustard
salt and pepper to taste

Don't be tempted to be stingy with the parsley. The sharp green color is half the pleasure of this dressing. We find it goes well with starch-rich vegetables like zucchini, or sweet vegetables like tomatoes or beets, or with pasta.

Place all the ingredients in a blender and blend first at medium speed and then at high speed until a smooth emulsion is achieved. Test the seasoning and adjust if necessary.

Mayonnaise

Mayonnaise A

1 large egg yolk
1 teaspoon Dijon mustard
a good pinch of salt
10 fluid ounces Italian extra
virgin olive oil or Provencal oil
lemon juice (up to 2 tablespoons)
to taste
additional salt and black pepper
to taste

Mayonnaise B

1 large egg
1 tablespoon prepared mustard
good pinch of salt
9 fluid ounces vegetable oil
wine vinegar (up to 2 tablespoons)
to taste
additional salt, black pepper,
paprika, or cayenne pepper
to taste

There is no mystique about making mayonnaise. You follow certain rules and in a few minutes there it is, thick enough for a mouse to jog on. Don't dream of buying it. Whatever you make and flavor it with is a matter of personal taste and consideration for the vegetables it is to accompany. For instance, fine delicate vegetables such as asparagus deserve a mayonnaise made from a light, cold-pressed virgin olive oil from Italy or Provence (method A). Mayonnaise to be thinned with yogurt for, say, a potato or cabbage salad should be made with the whole egg and peanut or sunflower oil (method B).

The Basic Rules

1. Mayonnaise is much easier to make with fresh eggs.
2. Ingredients and equipment must be warm. Some people warm everything in warm water.
3. At first, add the oil *very slowly* to the thickened egg.
4. Don't use less than 5 fluid ounces or more than 10 fluid ounces of oil per large egg.
5. The better the oil used, the less seasoning the mayonnaise will require.

Put the egg yolk (method A) or break the whole egg (method B) into a bowl or blender, and add mustard and salt. Beat or blend at medium speed until the mixture thickens slightly. Still beating, pour in the oil from a measuring cup, initially drop by drop, and then, as it begins to thicken, in a slow, but steady stream until all the oil is absorbed.

Carefully beat or blend in the lemon juice or wine vinegar and season to taste with the salt and pepper. Store in a cool place. Mayonnaise will keep for not much longer than a day.

MAYONNAISE VARIATIONS

The following are some of the possible ways of giving mayonnaise a different flavor. The amounts given are approximate. They are suitable for use with 5 fluid ounces mayonnaise.

CAPER

2 teaspoons chopped capers
1 teaspoon chopped pimiento
½ teaspoon tarragon vinegar
  Combine and serve.

CUCUMBER

2 tablespoons freshly chopped cucumber
½ teaspoon salt
  Combine and serve.

LEMON

rind of 1 lemon, finely grated
  Add grated rind and use lemon juice (same amount) instead of vinegar in the preparation of the mayonnaise. Combine and serve.

AÏOLI

2 cloves crushed garlic
  Combine and serve.

CELERY

1 tablespoon finely chopped celery
1 tablespoon finely chopped chives
  Combine and serve.

HERB

2 tablespoons freshly chopped chives
1 tablespoon freshly chopped parsley
  Combine and serve.

SPINACH

3 lightly blanched and finely chopped spinach leaves
1 tablespoon finely chopped parsley
2 tablespoons finely chopped chives
  Combine and serve.

Green Dressing

TO MAKE 10 FLUID OUNCES
OR 1¼ CUPS

**1 bunch of good fresh watercress,
  well washed**
1 tablespoon vegetable oil
**5 fluid ounces Mayonnaise
  (page 126)**
4 fluid ounces yogurt
salt and pepper to taste
**few growing tips of the watercress
  for garnish (optional)**

*This is a good, general-purpose sauce. You can use it on many
hot or cold young, tender vegetables and on cold white meats and fish.*

Trim the watercress of its roots and remove any discolored leaves.
Plunge the trimmed watercress into a pan of well salted boiling water
for little more than 10 seconds. This may seem a minor step, but it
does greatly enhance the color of the finished sauce.

Drain and refresh the watercress under cold running water until
it is quite chilled. Squeeze the watercress free of any excess water,
roughly chop it, place it in a blender with the oil, and blend it to
a smooth puree. Mix the watercress puree, the mayonnaise, and the
yogurt together in a small mixing bowl. Season to taste with salt
and pepper.

Strained Yogurt for Salad Making

MAKES ABOUT 1 CUP

*Thick yogurt is superior to the ordinary type for many salads and
very firm yogurt can also be eaten alone as an appetizer, see below.
Unfortunately, many commercial yogurts are often more than 50
percent whey or watery liquid, and they need to be strained and
thickened.*

*To do this, take a traditional jelly bag and pour into it 1 pint of
natural yogurt. Hang the bag over the sink or a large bowl and leave
it to drain overnight. In the morning, lightly press the yogurt and turn
it out into a bowl. It is now ready for use. A sieve lined with damp
cheesecloth can be used instead of a jelly bag.*

STRAINED YOGURT APPETIZER

Mix into the strained yogurt some chopped fresh herbs such as
chives, chervil, dill, parsley, or whatever you prefer or have available,
season it with salt and black pepper, dribble some olive oil over it,
and serve as a dip with raw vegetables or with hot pita bread.

Basic Tomato Sauce

MAKES 1 CUP

2 tablespoons olive oil
1 large shallot or ½ medium
    onion, very finely chopped
1 clove garlic, peeled and lightly
    crushed
1 medium can plum tomatoes,
    drained and roughly chopped
bouquet garni (½ bay leaf, sprig
    thyme, 4 parsley stems, tied in
    a 3-inch celery stick)
salt and pepper to taste
½ teaspoon fine sugar (optional)

This is a universal red sauce. You can make it in quantity and store it, soften it with cream, heat it up with hot chilies, enrich it with hazelnuts, add aromatic herbs, more garlic, paprika, sherry, or whatever you fancy. This sauce is good hot or cold.

Heat the oil in a medium saucepan over a low flame, add the chopped shallot or onion and the garlic clove and cook carefully for 5–7 minutes until the shallot or onion is soft but not browned. Stir in the chopped plum tomatoes, add the bouquet garni, turn heat to medium, and cook, covered, for 15–20 minutes. Check the sauce during this period and stir if necessary.

Remove the pan from the heat and remove the garlic clove and the bouquet garni. Season the sauce with salt and pepper and add the sugar, if desired.

Raw Tomato Sauce

18 ounces ripe tomatoes, skinned
    and seeded (see page 22)
1 tablespoon wine vinegar
2 tablespoons olive oil
1 tablespoon parsley, finely
    chopped
1 teaspoon dried oregano
salt and black pepper to taste

Use good, fresh, ripe tomatoes for the sauce. The skinning and the deseeding of the tomatoes are essential; but don't worry, it is a much simpler task than many people think.

Place all the ingredients in a blender and blend at low speed until a smooth sauce is obtained. Use the sauce over delicate vegetables, either as it is or thinned with whipping cream.

Rich Sweet and Sour Chili Dressing

MAKES 12 FLUID OUNCES

4 fluid ounces fresh orange juice
3 fluid ounces wine vinegar
3 fluid ounces tamari (natural
   soy sauce)
3 fluid ounces Basic Tomato Sauce
   (page 129)
2 tablespoons honey
2 teaspoons paprika
1 large clove garlic, peeled
1 almond-sized piece of ginger
   root, peeled
½–1 jalapeño chili pepper
salt to taste

This is an excellent, thick, dipping sauce for strips of carrot, cucumber, zucchini, sticks of celery, and florets of cauliflower. The same dressing can be used as a very fine marinade and sauce for barbecued pork ribs.

Place all ingredients in a blender, blend at medium speed until the solid ingredients have all been reduced, then blend at high speed for a further minute. Taste and adjust seasoning.

Speedy Chili Dressing

2 canned plum tomatoes, gently
   pressed free of juice
4 tablespoons vegetable oil
2 teaspoons hot pepper sauce
2 teaspoons tamari (natural soy
   sauce)

This chili dressing doesn't have the subtleties of the Rich Sweet and Sour Chili Dressing, but it is fresh, hot, and tangy. It is quick to make from items in the cupboard. Use it on green beans, snow peas, cooked dried beans, cauliflower, or broccoli.

Pour all the ingredients into a small, steep-sided mixing bowl and beat together with a fork or a small wire whisk.

Croûtons make good crunchy additions to leaf salads whether they be heavy-leaved red cabbage or light and delicate endives and icebergs.

You need good firm bread for making croûtons. A single ½-inch slice from a 2-pound loaf will make enough croûtons for 3–4 people.

Take a 5-inch pan and cover it to the depth of ½ inch with vegetable oil. Place the pan over medium heat. Meanwhile, remove the crusts from your slices of bread and cut into ½-inch cubes. When the oil has just begun to haze, test its temperature by dropping in one of the bread cubes. It should turn quite rapidly to a golden-brown color. Rescue the cube from the oil, reduce the heat slightly, and drop in enough of the bread cubes to loosely cover the bottom of the pan. Fry gently, turning them once. When the cubes are nicely browned all over, lift them out with a slotted spoon and drain them on paper towels. Repeat the process until all the bread is used.

These croûtons are best eaten fresh, but they will keep for a day or two in an airtight container.

VARIATION

Take a French loaf and cut it into ½-inch slices. Spread both sides of these slices with butter or brush them liberally with olive oil. Or spread on one side with thyme-flavored goat cheese or a mixture of equal quantities of Stilton and soft Camembert or pounded anchovies or anything of your creation. Lightly toast both sides of the bread under the broiler and serve.

Cream Dressing

MAKES 5 FLUID OUNCES

5 fluid ounces whipping cream
salt and cayenne pepper to taste
1–2 tablespoons wine vinegar

This rich dressing can be stored for up to 4 days in the refrigerator. Try it on fresh young vegetables like carrots, broad beans, broccoli, or new potatoes.

Season the cream to taste with salt and cayenne pepper. Whip it until nice and thick. Stir in the vinegar to taste gradually. Chill and serve.

Tofu (Bean Curd) Dressing

MAKES 1 CUP

6 ounces fresh tofu (bean curd),
**   drained**
1 tablespoon olive oil or other
**   vegetable oil**
1 tablespoon water
1 teaspoon lemon juice
1 teaspoon honey
salt to taste

Fresh white bean curd has the remarkable ability to carry a whole gamut of flavors. Blend it with a little liquid, add your flavoring— be it mustard, paprika, honey, shrimp paste, oyster sauce, whatever— and you have an instant low-fat "mayonnaise."

The central ingredient is so bland that these tofu dressings lack the intensity of flavor we prefer, but they do have a very high protein value and are very cheap to make. Here is a basic dressing; try it on crisp lettuce hearts.

Place all the ingredients in a blender or food processor. Blend together at high speed. Adjust seasoning.

Tahini Dressing

MAKES 14 FLUID OUNCES OR 1¾ CUPS

5 fluid ounces tahini (sesame paste)
5 fluid ounces natural yogurt
4 fluid ounces lemon juice
1–2 cloves garlic, crushed
3 tablespoons finely chopped parsley
½ teaspoon ground cumin or slightly less cayenne pepper
salt to taste

The most popular Middle-Eastern dressing. Tahini sauce can be poured over almost any fresh or cooked vegetables or served as a dip with hot bread. It is very simple and quick to make. The sauce can be thinned down, if it is overthick, with water or more yogurt. Tahini paste is produced by finely grinding sesame seeds. It is widely available in ethnic food stores and health-food shops.

Combine all the ingredients in a mixing bowl and beat together. Taste for seasoning.

Horseradish Sauce

MAKES 9 FLUID OUNCES

2 ounces peeled horseradish root
5 fluid ounces whipping or sour cream
2 tablespoons wine or cider vinegar
1 teaspoon sugar
½ teaspoon salt
½ teaspoon mustard powder (optional)

Horseradish is powerful stuff. If you are making this sauce entirely by hand, you would be wise to peel and grate the root out of doors. If you don't, be prepared for tears. A well controlled blender with a tight fitting lid will also make the preparation more pleasant. Horseradish sauce is good with beets, potatoes, or, less strongly flavored, with asparagus.

Blender method. Cut the horseradish root into small sections and place it together with the other ingredients in the blender or food processor. Replace the lid firmly, and blend first at low then higher speed, as the horseradish root is reduced, until the sauce is smooth. Chill before serving.
Hand method. Grate the horseradish root into a bowl. Lightly whip the cream and add it together with the rest of the ingredients to the horseradish. Stir thoroughly and chill before serving.

Hot Sweet and Sour Mango and Cilantro Dressing

MAKES ABOUT 5 FLUID OUNCES

**the leaves of half a bunch of
 cilantro, roughly chopped**
1 hot green chili, deseeded
1 clove garlic
1 walnut-sized piece of ginger
**1 tablespoon liquid from sweet
 mango chutney**
juice and pulp from 1 lemon
salt to taste

A delicious dressing of Indian origin that teases all the taste buds.

Blender method. Place all the ingredients in a blender or food processor and blend at high speed until a smooth sauce is achieved. Taste for salt.

Hand method. Finely chop the cilantro leaves and put them in a small mixing bowl. Crush the chili, garlic, and ginger through a coarse garlic press and add them to the cilantro. Add the rest of the ingredients. Beat together well and check the seasoning.

Poppy Seed Dressing

MAKES 5 FLUID OUNCES

**4 fluid ounces neutral vegetable
 oil (e.g., peanut or sunflower
 oil)**
2 tablespoons lemon juice
2 onion rings, roughly chopped
1 teaspoon poppy seeds
1 teaspoon cider vinegar
1 teaspoon honey

Poppy seeds may not transform the taste of a fruit salad, but they will give it a personality.

Place all the ingredients in a blender or food processor and blend at medium speed until the dressing is smooth.

Peanut Dressing

MAKES 12 FLUID OUNCES
OR 1½ CUPS

1 clove garlic, crushed
1 small onion, diced
1 tablespoon vegetable oil
4 ounces roasted unsalted
  peanuts or 4 ounces peanut
  butter
1 teaspoon brown sugar
1 tablespoon lemon juice
8 fluid ounces water
salt to taste

Serve this dressing hot or at room temperature on cooked and uncooked vegetable salads.

Lightly brown the garlic and onion in the oil. Transfer the garlic, onion, and frying oil to a blender or food processor and add all the other ingredients. Blend to a smooth mixture. Transfer the dressing to a pan, bring to the boil, and then simmer over a low heat, stirring for 5 minutes. Use immediately or allow to cool.

Cilantro Cream Sauce

MAKES 1¼ CUPS

1 bunch fresh cilantro
5 ounces cream
4 tablespoons neutral vegetable oil
  (e.g., sunflower or peanut)
2 tablespoons lemon juice
1 tablespoon French mustard
salt and black pepper to taste

A soft, mellow sauce that's good with eggs, pasta, salads, and white fish.

Wash the cilantro well and shake it dry. Cut away all but the finest stems. Place the trimmed leaves in a blender or food processor. Add the rest of the ingredients and blend well together at medium speed until a smooth green sauce is obtained. Test the seasoning.

Cheese Dressing

These cheese dressings are in many ways similar to the vinaigrette dressings, in that no one dressing is suitable for all occasions. You need delicate dressings for delicate produce and robust dressings for robust produce. Here are two extremes. Use or modify them to match your taste and requirements.

A MILD DRESSING
Use this on lettuce, celery, and Belgian endive.

MAKES 5 FLUID OUNCES

2 ounces crumbled Blue Stilton or
    finely diced firm Camembert
    or a mixture of both
4 fluid ounces light cream
1 tablespoon lemon juice
salt to taste
fresh chervil, chives, or dill
    for garnish

A STRONG DRESSING
Use this on red cabbage and chicory or escarole.

MAKES 5 FLUID OUNCES

2 ounces strong blue cheese,
    crumbled: Blue Cheshire,
    Shropshire Blue, or, if you can
    afford it, Roquefort
4 fluid ounces strong-flavored oil
    (e.g., olive or walnut)
2 tablespoons wine or cider
    vinegar
salt to taste
traditional croûtons (page 131),
    toasted sesame seeds for garnish

In both cases, combine the ingredients in a small mixing bowl and lightly beat them together with a small wire whisk. Taste and adjust seasoning.

Spicy Almond Dressing

MAKES 5 FLUID OUNCES

3 tablespoons sesame seeds
2 tablespoons coriander seeds
1 tablespoon cumin seeds
2 tablespoons flaked almonds
salt and cayenne pepper to taste

Many eastern countries—Egypt, India, Morocco, to name but three—have their dry savory dips. They vary from country to country, from family to family. Sesame and cumin seeds are featured in most of these, supported by coriander, chick-peas, hazelnuts, almonds, cayenne, and other ingredients. Roasting the seeds and nuts first is most important, as it really brings out the flavors, but do take care not to burn them. The mix may be made in quantity as it stores well in sealed jars. Here is a typical mixture.

Serve sprinkled over vegetable crudités, as a dip for bread, or just in place of salt and pepper.

Lightly dry-roast the seeds over a moderate heat in a small dry cast-iron frying pan. A French crêpe pan is very suitable. Stir constantly until lightly browned. Set aside to cool. Roast the nuts separately in a like manner. Grind the roasted seeds in a coffee grinder, mortar, or, briefly, an electric blender. Pour the ground seeds into a small mixing bowl with the toasted nuts, and season with salt and a touch of cayenne.

The appearance on the table of something unexpected like this, simple yet exotic, can make an ordinary meal into a feast.

Japanese Mustard Dressing

MAKES 4–5 TABLESPOONS

1 teaspoon prepared English
   mustard
2 tablespoons rice vinegar or
   cider vinegar
1 tablespoon tamari (natural soy
   sauce)
1–2 teaspoons sugar

Combine the mustard, vinegar, and tamari in a small mixing bowl, add sugar to taste, and stir well to dissolve the sugar.

Coconut Dressing

MAKES 1 CUP

4 ounces fresh coconut, grated,
   or 4 ounces dried coconut
   moistened with 2 tablespoons
   hot water
½ small onion, finely diced
pinch chili powder or ⅛ teaspoon
   hot pepper sauce
2 tablespoons lemon juice

A Southeast Asian dressing which is good on both cooked and uncooked vegetable salads.

Put all the ingredients into a blender or food processor and briefly blend to form a homogeneous but not completely smooth mixture.

Avocado Dressing

MAKES 1¼ CUPS

1 ripe avocado
1 tablespoon lemon juice
2 tablespoons Mayonnaise
(page 126)
2 tablespoons light cream
salt and freshly ground black
pepper

Excellent as a dip for raw vegetables.

Halve, pit, peel, and slice the avocado. Put the flesh into a blender or food processor with the remaining ingredients. Blend until velvety and smooth. Check the seasoning and use immediately.

Mexican Avocado Dressing

MAKES ABOUT 1¼ CUP

1 ripe avocado
1 hard-boiled egg, shelled
4 fluid ounces olive oil
3 tablespoons white vinegar
1 tablespoon tomato purée
½ teaspoon hot pepper sauce
salt to taste

A thick, spicy, hot dressing served on or with chopped raw vegetables such as carrots, young cauliflower, celery, and tender zucchini. For a thinner, less filling dressing, omit the boiled egg. For a milder or hotter dressing, adjust the amount of hot pepper sauce used.

Put the flesh of the avocado and the remaining ingredients into a blender or food processor and blend until the dressing is smooth.

Japanese White Dressing

MAKES 5 FLUID OUNCES

5-ounce cake of tofu (bean curd)
2 tablespoons sesame seeds
1 tablespoon white sugar
½ teaspoon salt

This has the consistency of mayonnaise and is used in Japanese cuisine as a dressing for raw and cooked salads. Make the dressing as needed; it doesn't keep well.

Remove excess water from the tofu in order to get a dressing of the right consistency. Wrap the tofu in 2 or 3 layers of absorbent paper towels and place a small bowl containing water on top of it. Leave for 30 minutes and then mash the pressed tofu in a bowl. Dry-roast the sesame seeds over a moderate heat until they are brown.

Crush the seeds into a paste with a mortar and pestle and stir the paste into the tofu. Add the sugar and salt and stir into a smooth consistency.

VARIATION

- The crushed sesame paste may be replaced by tahini or Chinese sesame paste.
- For Vinegared White Dressing, stir in 2 teaspoons rice or cider vinegar.

Ginger and Soy Sauce Dressing

MAKES 1 CUP

1 tablespoon peanut, sesame, or
  other vegetable oil
1 tablespoon finely grated ginger
  root
4 fluid ounces tamari (natural
  soy sauce)
4 fluid ounces water
1 tablespoon cider vinegar
1 clove garlic, crushed

A low-fat dressing for serving with lightly cooked vegetable salads, rice and bean salads, and root vegetable salads.

Combine the ingredients, mix well together, and leave to stand for 15–20 minutes before serving.

Sesame Seed and Soy Dressing

MAKES ½ CUP

4 tablespoons sesame seeds
1 teaspoon sugar
2 teaspoons tamari (natural
  soy sauce)
2 tablespoons water or stock
1 tablespoon rice vinegar or
  cider vinegar

4 tablespoons sesame seeds
4 tablespoons tamari (natural
  soy sauce)

The basic method given here is for a sweet-and-sour dressing best with crunchy, flavorful vegetables, while the variation, below, gives a nuttier-tasting, thicker dressing which goes well with softer-cooked vegetables like eggplant and zucchini. Tahini or Chinese sesame paste may be used in place of the sesame seeds.

Dry-roast sesame seeds over a moderate heat until they are golden brown. Crush the seeds into a paste with a mortar and pestle. Combine the paste with the remaining ingredients and mix well to dissolve the sugar.

VARIATION

Dry-roast and crush the sesame seeds as described above. Combine the sesame paste with the tamari and mix well.

Growing A Salad Garden

For the freshest vegetables possible, try growing your own in a *salad garden*—perhaps a small raised bed—just outside the kitchen door.

Plant ruby and green looseleaf lettuce, radishes, some onion sets, two pepper plants, two pixie tomato plants, two cucumbers (trained inside a wire cage), a few marigolds, and herbs such as basil, chives, parsley (curly and Italian), and thyme. Put poles of Kentucky Wonder beans at all four corners, and plant carrots around the tomatoes.

Place a couple of stepping stones in the center. Often-used herbs are just a snip away, and the palette of greens and varied textures makes a garden as eye-pleasing as any purely ornamental planting.

The ideal site for a vegetable garden should have:
- day-long sun (at least eight hours)
- good drainage (a slight slope to the south is perfect)
- protection from cold wind

Keep the garden away from tree roots, which will steal nutrients, and as close to the kitchen as practicable. You'll take better care of a garden that's near the house. You won't have to walk as far to and from the garden, so you'll go there more frequently, gather crops more conveniently, and be on the lookout for garden problems and pests.

If deer, rabbits, or pets are a problem, put a chicken-wire fence around your garden and train sugar snap peas to grow up it. Cucumbers can grow up the side of your house on a trellis.

Before planting your garden, prepare the soil by adding organic matter. This will improve the soil's physical condition and increase the

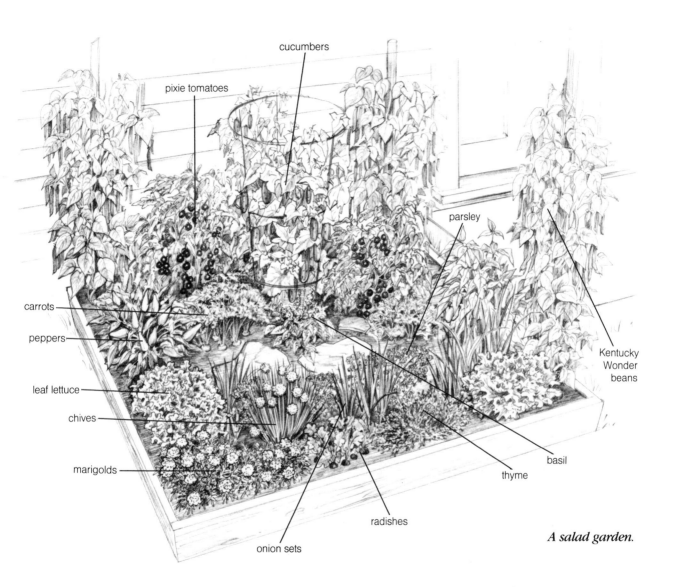

cucumbers

pixie tomatoes

parsley

carrots

peppers

leaf lettuce

chives

marigolds

Kentucky Wonder beans

basil

thyme

radishes

onion sets

A salad garden.

availability of nutrients to plants. Mix in compost or peat moss to a depth of four to six inches.

Test your soil to determine its degree of acidity or alkalinity, either through your County Extension Agent or a home test kit.

To make soil more acid, add elemental sulfur. One-third pound per twenty-five feet will lower pH one unit. To make soil more alkaline, add lime—one pound per twenty-five square feet to raise pH one unit. Wood ashes also increase the alkalinity of the soil. Use one-half pound per twenty-five square feet to raise pH one unit.

Plant cool-weather crops, like peas, lettuce, and onions, as soon as the soil is dry enough to crumble in your hand. Never work wet soil, especially clay, because you may ruin its structure and end up with solid, sun-baked clods later in the summer. Wait till the soil has warmed up before planting cucumbers, tomatoes, and peppers.

To save time and space, plant seed in broad bands the width of a rake, on beds that are built up six to ten inches above ground level. If you walk only on the stepping stones, and stay out of the planting area, your soil will remain spongy and fluffy, and may yield as much as four times more than planting in traditional narrow rows.

One easy way to plant a salad garden is to mix seeds of spinach, chard, assorted leaf lettuces, beets, and radishes in a bucket. Broadcast the seeds in the prepared bed and later thin with a rake.

The radishes are ready first—when you pull them, you make space. Next comes young spinach. Pull some of that to make space. From then on, just cut off the tops of everything for a continuous crop of greens. Plant a good-sized salad bed of this type in spring and two smaller ones during the summer. When the chard gets too big to eat raw, cook it.

Cover little seeds with compost when you plant, to hold moisture and provide a nutritional boost. Keep seedbed moist after planting.

The secret to weed control is to nab weeds when they're little, when it's easy to pluck them out. Later, when they're firmly rooted and threatening to take over the garden, eliminating them is hard work. With a small garden, you can weed for five or ten minutes every morning in spring. When summer comes, you'll only have to weed once a week at most.

Mulching—with hay or grass clippings, old newspapers (not color), pine needles, cocoa bean hulls, or wood chips—will smother weeds, retain moisture, and encourage the presence of earthworms.

When it comes time to harvest, pick your vegetables when they are small and tender, not stringy or tough. You'll have the satisfaction of knowing your own home grown vegetables are not only the freshest and most nutritious produce possible, but also the most delicious.

AVAILABILITY CHART

Shows when commercially marketed fresh fruits and vegetables are most plentiful nationwide and, therefore, cheapest. "Available Commercially" column indicates months when 1/12 or more of the annual crop reaches the market.

Fruit or Vegetable	Available Commercially	Peak Month(s)
Apples	Sept.-May	Oct.
Artichokes	Mar.-May	April
Asparagus	Mar.-June	April
Avocados:		
CA	Dec.-Aug.	Mar., June
FL	Aug.-Jan.	Oct.
Bananas	All year	
Beans, snap	April-Nov.	June
Beets	Feb.-Aug.	Mar.
Broccoli	Sept.-June	Nov.-May
Cabbage	Dec.-June	Mar.
Cantaloupe	June-Sept.	July, Aug.
Carrots	All year	Mar., April
Cauliflower	Sept.-May	Oct.
Celery	Nov.-July	Nov.
Chinese cabbage	Dec.-June., Aug., Sept.	Jan., Mar.
Cilantro (coriander)	All year	
Coconuts	Oct.-April	Dec.
Corn, sweet:		
FL	April-July	May, June
CA	May-Sept.	June
NY	July-Sept.	Aug.
Cucumbers	April-Aug., Oct., Nov.	June
Eggplant	All year	Jan.-June
Escarole/Endive	Dec.-May	April
Fennel	Sept.-May	Nov., Dec.
Garlic	All year	July-Aug.
Grapefruit:	Nov.-May	Mar.
FL	Oct.-May	Mar., April
TX	Nov.-April	Jan.
CA & AZ	May-Sept.	July
Grapes	July-Nov.	Aug.
Greens, misc.*	Dec.-May	Mar., April

*Includes beet tops, cabbage sprouts, collards, dandelion, mustard and turnip tops, kale, kohlrabi and rappini.

Fruit or Vegetable	Available Commercially	Peak Month(s)
Honeydews	June-Oct.	Sept.
Kiwifruit	All year	
Leeks	Feb.-June	May
Lemons	All year	May-July
Lettuce, iceberg	All year	May
Lettuce, romaine	All year	Jan., Mar.-May, Aug.
Lettuce, other	All year	Mar.-June
Limes	May-Oct., Dec.	July
Mushrooms	All year	
Okra	May-Oct.	Aug.
Onions	All year	
Onions, green	Nov.-July	Mar.-May
Oranges:	Dec.-May	Mar.-April
CA & AZ	Dec.-May	Mar., April
FL	Nov.-May	Dec.
Oriental vegs., misc.	All year	Jan., Feb.
Parsley	Aug.-April	Dec.
Parsnips	Oct.-April	Jan.
Pears	Aug.-Feb.	Oct.
Peas, green	Jan.-June	Mar.-May
Peppers, bell	All year	May, June
Pineapples	Jan.-July	May, June
Pomegranates	Sept.-Nov.	Oct.
Potatoes:	All year	
ID	Nov.-June	Mar., Apr.
CA	May-Aug.	June, July
Potatoes		
WA	Aug.-Nov.	Aug., Sept.
ME	Nov.-May	Mar., April
OR	Aug.-May	Jan.-May
Radishes	Nov.-May	May
Spinach	Oct.-June	Mar., April
Squash, all	April-Dec.	May, June
Strawberries:	Mar.-July	May
CA	April-July	May
FL	Jan.-April	April
Tangerines	Nov.-Mar.	Dec.
Tomatoes	Mar.-Oct.	May-July
Tomatoes, cherry	All year	June, July
Turnips & rutabagas	Sept.-April	Nov.
Watercress	All year	

Information courtesy of United Fresh Fruit and Vegetable Association, 1985 Supply Chart.

Index

Aïoli, 127
Almond
    dressing, spicy, 137
    and tahini dressing, apple and celery with,
        83
Appetizer(s)
    artichoke, 45
    nouvelle cuisine crudités, 60
    radishes served with aperitifs or as
        appetizer, 36
    salad *mezze*, 94
    strained yogurt, 128
Apple(s), 10
    carrot and, salad, 68
    and celery with almond and tahini
        dressing, 83
    fresh mint and, salad, 77
    and grapes with Japanese mustard
        dressing, 92
    Russian winter salad, 116
    spinach and, salad with lime dressing, 98
    stuffed, salad, 113
    sweet and sour celery and, salad, 82
    tomato, and watercress salad, 83
Apricots, four-color salad with Japanese
    white dressing, 70
Artichoke(s), 10–11
    appetizer, 45
Asparagus, 11
    with eggs mollet, 39
    with sesame seed and soy dressing, 51
Avocado(s), 11–12
    Belgian endive, and watercress salad in
        orange vinaigrette, 44
    dressing, 139
        Mexican, 139

Avocado(s) (*continued*)
    guacamole, 62
    and pink grapefruit salad, 48
    and red cabbage salad, 48
    snow pea and, salad, 46
    and yogurt salad, 49

Baby turnips in horseradish sauce, 44
Banana salad, celery and, 89
Basic tomato sauce, 129
Basil, 28–29
    tomatoes with, 69
Bean sprout(s). *See* Bean(s), sprout(s)
Bean(s)
    broad, 12
    brown rice and, salad, 120
    curd. *See* Tofu
    dried, 12
    gingered, 71
    green. *See* Green bean(s)
    kidney, salad, sweet corn and, 119
    navy
        in rich tomato sauce, 106
        salad, 85
    and pasta salad, 121
    sprout(s), 12
        kaleidoscope salad, 52
        and cucumber salad, 87
        mixed-up, salad, 95
        sweet and sour stir-fried salad, 118
    three-, salad, 114
    white, and sweet-sour beet salad, 109
Beet(s), 13
    four-root salad, 116
    greens, 25
    with horseradish cream, potato and, 119

Beets (*continued*)
    Russian winter salad, 116
    spiced, and walnut salad, 109
    sweet-sour, salad, white bean and, 109
    winter salad bowl, 98
Belgian endive, 24
    avocado, and watercress salad in orange
        vinaigrette, 44
    minted, salad, 43
Bibb lettuce, 24
Blue cheese dressing, creamy, 53
Bok choy, 24
Boston lettuce, 24
Broad beans, 12
Broccoli, 13–14
    with hot coconut sauce, 102
    with lemon egg mayonnaise, 46
Brown rice and bean salad, 120
Bulgur
    tabouli, 72

Cabbage, 14. *See also* Chinese cabbage
    coleslaw, 41
        in hot sour cream dressing, 100
    radish and, salad with chili dressing, 54
    red
        avocado and, salad, 48
        in juniper cream and yogurt sauce, 106
        walnut, fruit, and, salad, 99
    sweet and sour stir-fried salad, 118
    two-color, and tangerine salad, 101
Caraway, 32
Caribbean summer salad, 61
Carrot(s), 14–15
    and apple salad, 68

Carrot(s) (*continued*)
four-color salad with Japanese white
dressing, 70
four-root salad, 116
gingered, salad, 69
orange, date, and, salad, 104
orange and white vinegared salad, 110
and red currant salad, 68
Russian winter salad, 116
simple, salad, 60
Spice Street salad, 81
winter salad bowl, 98
Cauliflower, 15
salad, 85
Spice Street salad, 81
winter salad bowl, 98
Celeriac, 15
four-root salad, 116
remoulade, 50
Celery, 15–16
apple and, with almond and tahini
dressing, 83
and apple salad, sweet and sour, 82
and banana salad, 89
Cheese. *See also* specific cheeses
cooked pepper and, salad, 77
dressing, 136
salad with lime and yogurt dressing, 87
Chervil, 29
Chick-pea(s), 12
hot, salad, 115
Chicory, 24
with croûtons and sesame seeds, 40
and walnut salad, 50
Chili(es), 20
radish and cabbage salad with, dressing,
54
rich sweet and sour, dressing, 130
speedy, dressing, 130
Chinese cabbage, 24
and pomegranate in poppy seed dressing,
86
Chinese chard. *See* Bok choy
Chinese greens
with peanut dressing, 103
Chives, 29

Choi-sum. *See* Chinese greens
Cilantro, 29
cream egg salad, 42
cream sauce, 135
hot sweet and sour mango and, dressing,
134
leaves, fresh, spiced potato salad with, 51
Coconut
dressing, 138
sauce, hot, broccoli with, 102
Coleslaw, 41
in hot sour cream dressing, 100
Cooked pepper and cheese salad, 77
Coriander, 32
mushrooms, 90
Corn, 16
oil, 9
sweet, green beans and, with tomato
mayonnaise, 63
sweet, and kidney bean salad, 119
Corn salad. *See* Lamb's lettuce
Cos lettuce. *See* Romaine lettuce
Cottage cheese salad, 89
Cream dressing, 132
Cream sauce, cilantro, 135
Creamy blue cheese dressing, 53
Cress, 24
Croûton(s)
and sesame seeds, chicory with, 40
spinach, mushroom, and, salad, 105
traditional, 131
Crudités, nouvelle cuisine, 60
Cucumber(s), 16
bean sprout and, salad, 87
and cider salad, 67
kiwifruit, and pomegranate salad, 84
Mexican, 70
pear, grape, and, salad, 79
with sesame ginger dressing, 59
strawberry and, salad, 43
and thick yogurt dressing, 59
Cumin, 33
Curly endive. *See* Chicory
Currant, red, salad, carrot and, 68

Daikon. *See* Radish(es)

Dandelion, 24
Date
orange, and carrot salad, 104
parsnip and, salad, 103
Dill, 29–30
pea, and potato salad, 40
zucchini, and yogurt salad, 65
Dressing(s), 1–2, 124–141. *See also* Sauce
aïoli, 127
almond, spicy, 137
avocado, 139
Mexican, 139
cheese, 136
chili
rich sweet and sour, 130
speedy, 130
coconut, 138
cream, 132
creamy blue cheese, 53
egg and olive, 53
ginger and soy sauce, 141
green, 128
herb mayonnaise, 127
hot sweet and sour mango and cilantro,
134
Japanese mustard, 138
lemon mayonnaise, 127
mayonnaise, 126,
variations, 127
peanut, 135
poppy seed, 134
sesame seed and soy, 141
spinach mayonnaise, 127
tahini, 133
tofu, 132
vinaigrette, 125
green, 125
white, Japanese, 140

Egg(s)
cilantro cream, salad, 42
mayonnaise, lemon, broccoli with, 46
mollet, asparagus with, 39
and olive dressing, 53
spiced, and yogurt salad, 107

Eggplant, 16–17
  marinated, salad, 111
  ratatouille, 75
  spiced, salad, 74
Endive, Belgian. *See* Belgian endive
Endive, curly. *See* Chicory
Escarole, 24–25

Fava beans. *See* Bean(s), broad
Fennel, 17, 30
  cream dressing, Romaine salad in, 61
  and grapefruit salad, 36
  leek, and tomato salad, 101
Fig and walnut salad, winter, 105
Four-color salad with Japanese white
    dressing, 70
Four-root salad, 116
Fresh mint and apple salad, 77
Fruit
  availability chart, 146–147
  and vegetable yogurt salad, 93
  walnut, and red cabbage salad, 99

Gado-Gado, 123
Garlic, 17
Garnishes, 2
Ginger
  root, 34
  and soy sauce dressing, 141
  and yogurt rice salad, 95
Gingered beans, 71
Gingered carrot salad, 69
Grape(s)
  apple and, with Japanese mustard
      dressing, 92
  pear, and cucumber salad, 79
Grapefruit, 17
  pink, salad, avocado and, 48
  fennel and, salad, 36
Green bean(s)
  four-color salad with Japanese white
      dressing, 70
  simple, salad in lemon dressing, 63
  and sweet corn with tomato mayonnaise,
      63

Green Beans (*continued*)
  and tomato salad, 84
  tomato and, salad, 92
  winter salad bowl, 98
Green dressing, 128
Green garlic dressing, pasta with, 111
Green leaf salad, 97
Green tomato sauce, hot, tomatoes in, 86
Green vinaigrette dressing, 125
Guacamole, 62

Herb(s), 28–32. *See also* specific herbs;
  Spices
Horseradish
  cream, potato and beet with, 119
  cream sauce, baby turnips in, 44
  sauce, 133
  and soy sauce dressing, okra with, 64
Hot chick-pea salad, 115
Hot coconut sauce, broccoli with, 102
Hot green tomato sauce, tomatoes in, 86
Hot potato salad, 66
Hot sour cream dressing, coleslaw in, 100
Hot sweet-sour mango and cilantro dressing,
  134
Humus bi tahini, 91
Hyssop, 30

Iceberg lettuce, 25
Indian tomato salad, 76
Indonesian rice salad, 108

Japanese mustard dressing, 138
  apple and grapes with, 92
Japanese white dressing, 140
  four-color salad with, 70
Juniper, 33
  cream and yogurt sauce, red cabbage in,
  106

Kaleidoscope salad, 52
Kidney bean salad, sweet corn and, 119
Kitchen garden salad, 67
Kiwifruit, cucumber, and pomegranate
  salad, 84

Lamb's lettuce, 25
Leaf vegetables, 22–25
  green leaf salad, 97
Leek(s), 17–18
  fennel, and tomato salad, 101
  with sour cream dressing, 47
Lemon(s), 18
  dressing, simple green bean salad in, 63
  dressing, zucchini in olive oil and, 66
  egg mayonnaise, broccoli with, 46
  and mint dressing, spinach and walnut
      salad with, 49
  and yogurt dressing, new potatoes with
      spinach in, 37
Lentil(s), 12
  salad, rice and, 122
Lettuce, 22–25. *See also* Leaf vegetables;
  specific varieties
Lime(s), 18
  dressing, spinach and apple salad with, 98
  and yogurt dressing, cheese salad with, 87
Looseleaf lettuce, 25

Mango and cilantro dressing, hot sweet and
    sour, 134
Marinated eggplant salad, 111
Marjoram, 30
Mayonnaise, 126
  lemon egg, broccoli with, 46
  tomato, green beans and sweet corn with,
      63
  variations, 127
Mexican avocado dressing, 139
Mexican cucumber, 70
Mezze, simple salad, 94
Mint, 30
  fresh, and apple salad, 77
  and lemon dressing, spinach and walnut
      salad with, 49
Minted Belgian endive salad, 43
Minted new potatoes with parsley
    vinaigrette, 38
Mixed-up bean sprout salad, 95
Moroccan cooked salad, 88
Mushroom(s), 18
  coriander, 90

Mushrooms (*continued*)
spinach, and croûton salad, 105
Mustard, 25, 33
dressing, Japanese, 138
apple and grapes with, 92

Navy bean(s)
in rich tomato sauce, 106
salad, 85
New potatoes with spinach in lemon and
yogurt dressing, 37
Nouvelle cuisine crudités, 60

Oils, 8–9
Okra with horseradish and soy sauce
dressing, 64
Olive
dressing, egg and, 53
oil, 8
and lemon dressing, zucchini in, 66
Onion(s), 18
spiced yogurt and, salad, 112
Orange and white vinegared salad, 110
Orange(s), 18–19
date, and carrot salad, 104
vinaigrette, Belgian endive, avocado, and
watercress salad in, 44
Oregano, 30–31

Pantry essentials, 26–27
Paprika potatoes, 82
Parsley, 31
green vinaigrette dressing, 125
vinaigrette, minted new potatoes with,
38
zucchini and, salad, 64
Parsnip
and date salad, 103
four-root salad, 116
Pasta
bean and, salad, 121
with green garlic dressing, 111
Pea(s)
green, 19
and potato salad, dill, 40
snap, 19

Peas (*continued*)
snow, and avocado salad, 46
winter salad bowl, 98
Peanut
dressing, 135
Chinese greens with, 103
oil, 9
sauce, in Gado-Gado, 123
Pear(s), 19
grape, and cucumber salad, 79
Pepper (spice), 33
Pepper(s). *See also* Chili(es)
cooked, and cheese salad, 77
hot, 20
sauce, 34
sweet, 19–20
kaleidoscope salad, 52
red, salad, 76
and tomato cream salad, 80
sweet and sour stir-fried salad, 118
Peppercress. *See* Cress
Pineapple(s), 20
kaleidoscope salad, 52
Pomegranate(s), 20
Chinese cabbage and, in poppy seed
dressing, 86
salad, cucumber, kiwifruit and, 84
Poor boy salad, 58
Poppy seed dressing, 134
Chinese cabbage and pomegranate in, 86
Potato(es), 20–21
and beet with horseradish cream, 119
dill, pea, and, salad, 40
hot, salad, 66
new
minted, with parsley vinaigrette, 38
with spinach in lemon and yogurt
dressing, 37
paprika, 82
Russian winter salad, 116
spiced, salad, with fresh cilantro leaves, 51
short eats, 73

Radicchio, 25
Radish(es), 21
and cabbage salad with chili dressing, 54

Radish(es) (*continued*)
four-color salad with Japanese white
dressing, 70
orange and white vinegared salad, 110
served with aperitifs or as appetizer, 36
watercress and, salad, 52
Ratatouille, 75
Raw tomato sauce, 129
Red cabbage. *See also* Cabbage
avocado and, salad, 48
in juniper cream and yogurt sauce, 106
walnut, fruit, and, salad, 99
Red currant salad, carrot and, 68
Rice
brown, and bean salad, 120
ginger and yogurt, salad, 95
Indonesian, salad, 108
and lentil salad, 122
sushi, salad, 112–113
Rich sweet and sour chili dressing, 130
Romaine lettuce, 25
salad in fennel cream dressing, 61
Russian winter salad, 116

Safflower oil, 9
Salad garden, growing, 142–145
Salad making, general guidelines, 3–4
Sauce. *See also* Dressing(s)
cilantro cream, 135
horseradish, 133
tomato, basic, 129
tomato, raw, 129
Sesame
ginger dressing, cucumber with, 59
oil, 8
paste. *See* Tahini
seed and soy dressing, 141
asparagus with, 51
spinach with, 93
Short eats, potato, 73
Simple carrot salad, 60
Simple green bean salad in lemon dressing,
63
Smothered salads, 53
Snap peas. *See* Pea(s), snap
Snow pea and avocado salad, 46

Sour cream dressing, leeks with, 47
Sour cream dressing, hot, coleslaw in, 100
Soy dressing, sesame seed and, 141
Soy oil, 9
Soy sauce
    ginger and, dressing, 141
    horseradish and, dressing, okra with, 64
Speedy chili dressing, 130
Spice Street salad, 81
Spiced beet and walnut salad, 109
Spiced egg and yogurt salad, 107
Spiced eggplant salad, 74
Spiced potato salad with fresh cilantro
    leaves, 51
Spiced yogurt and onion salad, 112
Spices, 32–33. See also Herbs; specific spices
Spicy almond dressing, 137
Spinach, 25
    and apple salad with lime dressing, 98
    in lemon and yogurt dressing, new
        potatoes with, 37
    mushroom, and croûton salad, 105
    with sesame seed and soy dressing, 93
    and walnut salad with mint and lemon
        dressing, 49
Spring, fruits and vegetables, 35
Sprouts. See Bean(s), sprout(s)
Stir-fried salad, sweet and sour, 118
Strained yogurt, 128
Strawberry and cucumber salad, 43
Stuffed apple salad, 113
Sugar snaps. See Pea(s), snap
Summer
    green salad, 57
    herbs, 56
Sunflower oil, 9
Sushi rice salad, 112–113
Sweet corn and kidney bean salad, 119
Sweet pepper and tomato cream salad, 80
Sweet red pepper salad, 76
Sweet and sour celery and apple salad, 82
Sweet and sour chili dressing, rich, 130
Sweet and sour stir-fried salad, 118
Sweet-sour beet salad, white bean and, 109

Tabouli, 72

Tahini, 34
    dressing, almond and, apple and celery
        with, 83, 133
    humus bi, 91
Tamari. See Soy sauce
Tangerine salad, two-color cabbage and, 101
Tarragon, 31
Thick yogurt dressing, cucumber with, 59
Three-bean salad, 114
Thyme, 31–32
Tofu
    dressing, 132
    vegetable and, salad, 117
Tomato(es), 21–22
    apple, and watercress salad, 83
    with basil, 69
    cream salad, sweet pepper and, 80
    fennel, leek, and, salad, 101
    green bean and, salad, 84
    and green bean salad, 92
    in hot green tomato sauce, 86
    Indian, salad, 76
    mayonnaise, green beans and sweet
        corn with, 63
    sauce
        basic, 129
        hot green, tomatoes in, 86
        raw, 129
        rich, navy beans in, 106
Traditional croûtons, 131
Turnips, baby, in horseradish cream sauce,
    44
Two-color cabbage and tangerine salad, 101

Vegetable
    availability chart, 146–147
    and tofu salad, 117
    yogurt salad, fruit and, 93
Vinaigrette
    dressing, 125
        green, 125
    orange, Belgian endive, avocado, and
        watercress salad in, 44
    parsley, minted new potatoes with, 38
Vinegars, 9

Walnut
    chicory and, salad, 50
    fruit, and red cabbage salad, 99
    oil, 9
    spiced beet and, salad, 109
    spinach and, salad with mint and lemon
        dressing, 49
    winter fig and, salad, 105
Watercress, 25
    Belgian endive, avocado, and, salad in
        orange vinaigrette, 44
    green dressing, 128
    kaleidoscope salad, 52
    and radish salad, 52
    tomato, apple, and, salad, 83
White bean and sweet-sour beet salad, 109
White dressing, Japanese, 140
Wild marjoram. See Oregano
Winter
    fig and walnut salad, 105
    Russian, salad, 116
    salad bowl, 98

Yogurt
    avocado and, salad, 49
    fruit and vegetable, salad, 93
    lemon and, dressing, new potatoes with
        spinach in, 37
    lime and, dressing, cheese salad with, 87
    rice salad, ginger and, 95
    sauce, juniper cream and, red cabbage in,
        106
    spiced, and onion salad, 112
    spiced egg and, salad, 107
    strained, 128
    thick, dressing, cucumber with, 59
    zucchini, dill, and, salad, 65

Zucchini, 22
    dill, and yogurt salad, 65
    in olive oil and lemon dressing, 66
    and parsley salad, 64
    ratatouille, 75

Other Books
You Will Enjoy

The Apple Cookbook, by Olwen Woodier. 156 pages, quality paperback, 0-88266-367-4. $6.95.

Grow Your Own Chinese Vegetables, by Geri Harrington. 124 pages, quality paperback, 0-88266-369-0. $7.95.

Growing and Using Herbs Successfully, by Betty E.M. Jacobs. 240 pages, quality paperback, 0-88266-249-X. $8.95.

Joy of Gardening Cookbook, by Janet Ballantyne. 336, pages, quality paperback, 0-88266-355-0. $17.95.

Simply Strawberries, by Sara Pitzer. 123 pages, quality paperback, 0-88266-382-8.

Tips for the Lazy Gardener, by Linda Tilgner. 124 pages, quality paperback, 0-88266-390-9. $4.95.

The Zucchini Cookbook and Other Squash, by Nancy C. Ralston and Marynor Jordan. 144 pages, quality paperback, 0-88266-107-8. $5.95.

These books are available at your bookstore, or may be ordered directly from Garden Way Publishing, Schoolhouse Road, Pownal, Vermont 05261. Please add $2.00 for postage and handling.